Where Fear Rules

Fear is the opposite of faith

Fear says you can't, it doesn't trust.
It hinders, weakens and debilitates.
Faith says you can,
even when you cannot see or understand.
Faith trusts God.
It allows, authorises and empowers.

Written by Janene Forlong
Illustrated by Kimberley Williamson

Where Fear Rules

Copyright © 2016 Janene Forlong
First published November 2016
Second Edition April 2022
ISBN 978-0-473-37471-6
Printed by: www.yourbooks.co.nz

This book is copyright.
Apart from any fair dealing for the purpose of
private study, research, criticism or review,
as permitted under the Copyright Act,
no part may be reproduced by any process
without permission of the publisher.

A dedication to my beautiful Mum, Mary Hilton

Love you so much!

Contents

1. Foreword — 9
2. Endorsement — 11
3. Acknowledgements — 13
4. Introduction — 15
5. **Chapter 1** Where Fear Rules — 19
6. **Chapter 2** The Road to Fear — 33
7. **Chapter 3** Fear and Friends — 41
8. **Chapter 4** What the Bible Says... — 53
9. **Chapter 5** Why Choose Freedom — 63
10. **Chapter 6** Flight to Freedom — 73
11. **Chapter 7** Weapons of Warfare — 85
12. **Chapter 8** Where Freedom Rules — 101
13. **Chapter 9** Freedom and Responsibility — 111
14. Freedom Toolbox — 121
15. Scriptures for Healing and Deliverance — 123
16. Fear Eviction Plan — 129

Foreword

When Janene asked if I would write a foreword for her latest literary venture I had no hesitation in saying yes, even before reading 'Where Fear rules', because I believed from how she described the project, that it was God inspired. Having now 'devoured' every page I am pleased to recommend it to the many Christian brothers and sisters, who for probably a myriad of reasons, still find themselves under the sometimes-crippling influence of fear and anxiety.

What Janene has undoubtedly achieved, is not only a comprehensive 'self-help book' based heavily on the word of God, but equally relevant from her own life's journey and personal experiences. I've often said, that it is very hard to understand the power and influence of personal testimony and indeed, in the case of "Where Fear Rules" its input is vital for us to understand and identify the many aspects of fear in the many lives in the church today.

At this point, I think it is also helpful perhaps, to mention that for a significant part early in my own 30 plus years as a committed Christian, I experienced what can only be described as totally debilitating, immobilising bondage to fear. Even to the point of not being able to leave my own driveway to venture out into society. Let me say that the 'help' outlined in Janene's book was similar to my own journey to freedom in Christ to the degree of being able to achieve some special parts of my own God-given destiny while at the same time understanding more fully the grace and love of God.

As I have, after reading this book, I hope you also will grasp more firmly how a loving God sees each of us and that within that – fear has no place! Galatians 2:20

Wayne R Douglas
Radio/TV Broadcaster/Friend

"There are some things that are too personal and painful to share with others, but not with Janene. In this book she describes how she faced her debilitating fears head on, and saw them as a ploy of the enemy to rob her of her personal fulfilment and joy. She discovered in God's Word, the keys that would bring her victory and freedom in these areas. As you read her story you will be inspired, and should you become aware of fears that negatively impact your life, you too can use these same keys to set yourself free."

Stuart Forlong
Pastor, Helensville Christian Life Centre

"This book is a testimony to Janene's inner strength. She has carried the burden of fear for too many years. Her song writing has always inspired me and now with this book, my prayer is that many who have been crippled by fear might find freedom."

Annie Hilton
Freeset

"This book will certainly be a great help to those who are living with a degree of fear in their lives. Janene speaks from the heart and shares details that draw the reader in. The practical and God-centred advice is genuine and authentic."

Heather Claycomb
Founder/Director
HMC Communications

"Synonyms for *"fear"* and *"being afraid"* are a frequent theme throughout the Bible, usually prefaced by the injunction *"do not."* Sometimes this can be cold comfort for those gripped within its grasp. Janene Forlong is a wonderful friend and colleague and writes in practical and approachable terms about her own journey into, and out of, fear's control over her life. This is not so much a technical book written for academics, analysing fear in all its nuances and manifestations. It's more a compelling story of one woman's experience in allowing God to bring healing and hope over an illegal ruler. Easy to identify with, and supremely practical in its application, you'll find this book helpful in dislodging the negative power of fear, replacing it with God's perfect love and all the hope he delights to give us."

Brian Winslade
Pastor
Hamilton Central Baptist Church

"'Where Fear Rules' is a much-needed book for our times. It comes from the heart of one who has experienced deeply the grace of Christ and who longs to see others freed from the destruction fear causes. It is a book which will not only provide a pathway for sufferers of fear to explore and discover Christ's freedom for themselves; it is also a wise and wonderful resource for those engaged in the pastoral care of others."

Ian Brown, Pastor, Baptist Churches, New Zealand

"I remember my little sister struggling with so much fear. The sister I now have is free and seeing the world in all its vibrant colour. Real freedom is never something we keep to ourselves but rather is shared with anyone who will listen. This book is Janene's way of saying "here's how you can be free too" recognising ultimate freedom is found in Jesus. Proud of you Sis."

Kerry Hilton, Freeset

"In this insightful but easy to read book, Janene has tackled the big subject of fear with honesty, integrity and optimism. Combining practical tools with strong scriptural backing this book provides a comprehensive framework in which to find a level of freedom that will bring about real change. I highly recommend it both as reading material and a practical toolkit."

Juliagrace
Singer, Speaker, Storyteller

Acknowledgments

My greatest acknowledgement and thanks must be to Jesus who has healed and restored me so beautifully and fully. I can now experience the abundant life He has promised me right here in this life and onwards into eternity.

Michael Forlong and I were married while I was still very broken, hurting and fearful and yet he was the perfectly caring and loving husband who not only showed me not to fear but helped me realise that I could be free. Thank you Michael for being the gentleman and the help mate that I needed. It can't have been easy for you at times but you stood by me and loved me through it all.

Thank you Josiah and Tamsyn for your constant love, honour and support, I feel so very privileged to be your mother and I am so proud of who you both have become.

Mum and Dad you have been there for me through some of the darkest times in my life. I often look back at how we were living in the same city during some of my most difficult times and how that had to have been organised by Father God. Thank you for the prayer, love and constant support.

Stuart and Prue Forlong thank you for believing in me, taking me in as your daughter-in-law and praying for me. I appreciate your time and support in helping me put this book together, I think I might just have the best parents-in-laws ever!

Heather Claycomb, thank you for your generous support, wonderful friendship and professional expertise.

Thank you Dr Coral Dixon for expressing interest in the content of this book and for writing to endorse the complicating issue that stress plays in our lives, particularly to do with our health.

Kerry and Annie Hilton, Wayne Douglas, Ian Brown, Brian Winslade and JuliaGrace, thank you for the encouragement you gave me through the writing and publishing process. Your support helped me write and share my heart with others, with the hope that they too will find freedom.

Kimberley Williamson, wow what a talent! So good working with you on this project, love your work and I appreciate the time, passion and effort you put into it all.

Introduction

So, you are no longer a slave,
but God's child;
and since you are His child,
God has made you also an heir.

Galatians 4: 7

Fear isn't always bad; there is healthy fear and unhealthy fear. We should have a healthy fear of God and, quite naturally, if there is danger a healthy fear assists us with survival. There is also the neutral kind of fear, you know, "no worries, be happy." It is the fear that debilitates, weakens and incapacitates us that is of concern. This kind of fear alarms us, causing trembling, phobias and paranoia.

I wanted to write this book because it troubles me to see people handicapped and enslaved by fear. It is so terribly debilitating and, without God it is completely impossible to break free.

Fear is rampant right across the globe. We have all experienced it to some degree, but the fact is, God did not give fear to us and never intended for us to be held back by it. He created us to be free, calls us to a life of liberty and He has made a way for us to journey back to freedom if we are lost in fear.

I know all about fear as I struggled for years just to be myself with friends, family, work colleagues and even serving in church. I am experiencing a huge amount of freedom now, but I also understand there is more freedom to come. Of course, it is no longer so frightening to face or conquer the fear as the most difficult part of my journey to freedom is complete.

The thing that I have learned most from this long journey is, that I am overwhelmingly loved by an amazing God, my Heavenly Father. His Word is absolute truth. It is so easy to say or write these things down but to really believe them in the very core of your spirit is another thing. I am what He says I am, not what others say and not what 'I think' others are saying. I am safe and secure.

If you are living with fear you may feel a bit uncomfortable as you read this book but please do not allow negative thoughts to prevent you from learning what you desperately need to know. I encourage you to read with an open mind and allow God to show you any areas of fear you have. It can only mean more freedom for you even if you already have some degree of release.

I have shared a lot of my own personal journey here with the hope that you may identify with at least some of it. This book could also be helpful for those who have friends or family living with fear. The knowledge you gain will help you to understand them better, allowing you to effectively care for them and pray for them.

How this book works

We will start by looking at what fear looks like when it is ruling, then we will go down the road to find out how we got into the state we are in. We take a look at how fear can grow into something much bigger than we ever expected and then we will look at the options we have – stick with fear or fight for freedom. Checking out what the Bible says will be really helpful and then we will roll over to chapter six, which could be the perfect tool box for evicting fear. After that we look at the free life, how to keep the freedom and what responsibilities come with this new found liberty.

If you want to write in the book to help yourself with your journey to freedom, I have created some space for you titled, 'Your Reflections.' You can write your answers to all the bulleted questions there, at the end of each chapter.

At the back of the book, there are some scriptures for you to declare, these will be helpful during your flight to freedom. So, enjoy the read but make sure you give yourself some time to digest it all.

Chapter 1:
Where Fear Rules

Always trying to make things look pretty.
Always covering up the truth.
The birds in the sky, you see what they are,
but me, who can see?
A wall between my words and me.
A face that does not show anymore
than what I want people to see,
me, who can see?

Janene Forlong 1981

Living with fear can be extremely debilitating, and it is one thing to know that you are fearful and another to realise you have the fear enslaved lifestyle and believe it to be normal.

I began to understand that I had some abnormal fear but I was unaware of the degree of fear I was dealing with on a daily basis. After many years of living with fear I was also afraid to be free. I guess you could say, I was co-dependent on the feeling of fear that had become so familiar to me. I began to justify my behaviours and pretensions to myself and to my family just so I could keep things the way they were.

As I look around at my friends, family and community now, through the eyes of someone who has battled and dealt with a lot of fear, I am amazed at the amount of people enslaved with this horrid thing and unaware of the fact. What saddens me even more, is that many of these people are Christian. These are the very ones that should be free or at least aware they are enslaved and proactively on the journey to freedom.

Right now, you may think you have no fear or very little and I wonder, will you think the same way a few pages or chapters into this book? I believe it is important to understand what life is like 'with fear' and what it is like 'without.' It is essential to make sure you have the power to choose how you would like to live your life: with fear or without.

We are all vulnerable to fear, but there are several ways it enters our lives and most often without us being aware it has 'taken up residence.' We either inherit fear or it enters circumstantially through trauma, grief, high levels of stress or an illness of some kind.

Fear is a state of unpleasant or disturbing feelings induced by perceived danger. It is developed as a result of learning; in other words, we learn to be afraid through our own life experiences or by watching or hearing from someone else. Some fear is natural, even helpful as part of our survival skills. The problem with fear is when it begins to rule and determine our life story making it difficult to reach our potential or even enjoy life.

To live with fear means your mindset and perspective on life is vastly different to someone without fear, almost as if you are looking through completely different lenses at the exact same thing at the same time. Fear disables our emotions and our will; we are unable to make the choices and decisions we would make if we were otherwise free.

Ask yourself a few questions...

- ❖ Are you honestly free to <u>really live</u>?
- ❖ Are you able to achieve what you were created and designed for? What is stopping you?
- ❖ Are your day-to-day decisions controlled or impacted by what you are afraid of or worried about?

Your honest answers to these questions may help you uncover any fear you may have, if you do not already know. As you keep reading you may discover what level of fear you are dealing with and how much it is ruling your life.

I chose the title, 'Where Fear Rules', because just having the knowledge of what it is like where fear rules can empower and propel us towards freedom. Another reason is because most of my life fear has ruled, but now I am experiencing freedom. Life is so much more meaningful and enjoyable when my decisions are not made through the eyes of fear or because of it.

For many of us, our experience is that the homes we grew up in were a place where fear ruled, so we subconsciously imitated the habitual behaviours set up by our parents and siblings. We then make a subconscious choice to carry these familiar traits into our adult lives. For many of us living in fear has always been normal and familiar. We didn't live in a family where it was different, so why would we question it?

But there are those who have been through traumatic life experiences and no matter what age these events took place, our response can be to react in fear by forming new habits that we think will protect us. We allow fear to choose and decide how things will be from then on because we don't have the knowledge or the understanding at the time to consider what other options we have. Whatever our life's journey, many of us find ourselves here, *'where fear rules.'*

Fear saps the strength of anyone trying to live with it, debilitating them with low self-esteem, often to the point of suspicion and paranoia. Some fear produces an instant bodily response. You may have noticed these kinds of signs or symptoms in yourself or someone else.

- Accelerated breathing rate or heart rate
- Blushing
- Goosebumps
- Sweating
- Increased muscle tension
- Sleep disturbance
- Butterflies in the stomach
- Excessive alertness

It is good to remember that anxiety is a feeling of fear, rather than fear itself. There are different levels of fear as well as numerous things people are afraid of.

Check out this list of common fears:

- Fear of abandonment
- Fear of being alone
- Fear of being touched
- Fear of commitment
- Fear of change
- Fear of clowns
- Fear of crowds
- Fear of death, dying
- Fear of dentists
- Fear of doctors
- Fear of dogs
- Fear of driving
- Fear of engulfment
- Fear of failure
- Fear of falling
- Fear of flying
- Fear of germs
- Fear of girls
- Fear of God
- Fear of heights
- Fear of intimacy
- Fear of men
- Fear of needles
- Fear of open spaces
- Fear of public speaking
- Fear of rejection
- Fear of snakes
- Fear of spiders
- Fear of the dark
- Fear of thunder
- Fear of water

Ask yourself these questions…

- ❖ Do you have any body responses when you are afraid?
- ❖ Do you have any of these fears listed?
- ❖ Do you have fears that are not included on this list?

Having lived many years experiencing at least 15 of the above common fears, plus a few more, I can tell you this meant life was not as enjoyable as it should have been. It led me to too many no's and can't do's! It led me to avoiding, preventing and procrastinating. The boundaries and walls that I put up and the decisions I made, were all wrapped up and set by my fears; I was shut into a small-minded lifestyle.

My personal fear-induced lifestyle was a result of two scenarios, what was familiar to me and the trauma I had experienced. I grew up with some fear in my household, so fearful feelings and the behaviours that generally accompany them were far too familiar to me. Knowing that we teach our children our behaviours and responses, I cannot blame my parents for my fears, as I have done the same thing to my own children.

I wonder now, if because fear was already familiar to me as a young child, that when I went through trauma the natural thing to do was to go with the familiar feelings and responses, making the decisions that I thought would best protect me.

The traumatic life experience that had the biggest impact on me was a nasty occurrence when I was six years old. At the time it happened, I went into such shock that I was unable to tell my parents exactly what had taken place. They dealt with the situation as best they could with the limited information they had. They never knew the full details until I was an adult and free to explain. It was years later, when I finally said out loud to someone that I was sexually abused that day. Despite the seemingly small level of abuse, in comparison to many others' experiences, the impact was still great because of my age at the time. Looking back now I can see how this horrible event damaged me. I was afraid of men, intimacy, physical touch, rejection, germs, doctors, failure and so much more. Of course, there were many other life experiences that added to the above trauma over time, things that life hands out to all of us.

I am now going to talk about a few specific and common fears to create a bit of a picture of what it can look like when fear is ruling.

Fear of Man
A stranger sexually abused me, but after the event I was generally afraid and uncomfortable with most men. Those that were warmer and caring were easier to trust but it always took me a while to feel safe with them.

Men in authority positions were the hardest for me to trust and unfortunately I had some other common life experiences that compounded the issue through school and my early work life. These issues included things like an overly harsh male teacher and principal at primary school and a difficult male boss in one of my first jobs.

This all meant that though I was very capable, I did not come across well at times because I was afraid, insecure and not at all confident. I found it hard to speak to people over the phone. I would never approach someone I didn't know, shyness being part of that issue but not all. I was unable to deal with a concern if it meant talking to a man, so things remained unsaid and unchallenged and without closure.

Fear of Intimacy
It is a very sad thing to look hopefully forward to the wonderful things that marriage can bring, in the way of friendship, love and intimacy. Only to find that when you finally get married, you discover you have a fear of intimacy. This is clearly linked to the traumatic experience I had when I was six, but exacerbated by other painful events that took place. This has been a really immense issue for me; it affected my marriage, my family and my

friendships. I am very blessed though, to have such a caring and understanding husband who has stood by me through all this. At the time of writing this book we have been married twenty-nine years and going strong.

Fear of Rejection

I do not remember a time when I was not afraid of what others thought of me. The horrible tangled web of worry and expectation that people will reject and not accept me, because of what I say, look like, or they simply don't understand me. This fear leads into the habit of needing to impress particular people with the hope they will accept me and make me feel good about myself.

But this kind of behaviour only ended in deep emotional pain, because whether these people showed obvious signs of acceptance or rejection, I would read and deduct from their actions and language that I had again failed to make and maintain a good impression. This is a raging, emotional, vicious cycle, one that is a lot more rampant across humankind than we care to realise.

Fear of Germs

I had struggled with the fear of germs on and off during my adult life. The most recent time, was only about five years ago and this time I understood it was abnormal. I didn't like it, didn't want it and was unaware of how to get rid of it. I had seen it in others and I knew the debilitating impact it can have. It made it quite difficult for me to go on holiday at any time, to any place. I always felt uncomfortable in other people's homes, in motels and camping grounds, so it was just easier to stay home and not to have to deal with the issues I faced when away. I didn't trust others to have a realistic level of hygiene and I was certainly able to explain why they should be more cautious not just for me, but for others also.

This fear began to rule when I was quite unwell. Fear often creeps in when people are sick as they are more vulnerable at that time. Five years ago, my health was at an all-time low but it had gone downhill slowly, so I hadn't realised how poorly I was. One of the ways I handled this fear was to do almost everything myself, so that I didn't have to be concerned about how others may be contaminating me. What a terrible way to live life!

Fear of Failure

Right from a young age, I didn't believe that I would ever achieve much of any value. I had believed a negative phrase spoken to me by someone who honestly thought they were being funny. The phrase was repeatedly spoken over a few years, it went right into my spirit and became the truth to me. If the person realised what they had done, they would be horrified, I am sure. But the impact was big and it has taken a long time to deal with.

I do love to do things really well and I take pride in doing so, but the need to be and do things perfectly often makes it hard for me to accept when I do something that is clearly not good enough. The downside to perfectionism coupled with insecurity, is that I developed a strong need to impress others and receive affirmation. This unrealistic expectation can lead to a rocky emotional life.

Stress

Stress is a state of mental and emotional strain caused by long term or high-level adverse circumstances. When we live with constant and noticeable levels of fear we will generally begin to openly display mental tension. This kind of tension would more often than not manifest itself as stress and it is one of our body's responses to fear and emotional pain.

For example, we may fear our own or another's inability to efficiently accomplish an outcome in the time given, or with the resources available. Our work load may be hugely unrealistic or we may just perceive it is, either way our stressed responses are a reaction to what we fear may happen. When we are deeply rooted in stress it could be true that our ability to accurately gauge what is realistic is now unreliable.

When we are under excessive stress over long periods of time, it can impact our physical and mental health: in-fact a very high percentage of sickness arises from stress, anxiety and fear. There are many illnesses that have confirmed links to stress such as the common cold, angina, high blood pressure, stroke, heart attacks, weight gain, cancer, lung disease, cirrhosis of the liver, mental illness, impotence, gum disease and premature aging.

The fact that chronic stress is a key factor contributing to the development of many modern diseases is well recognised and acknowledged by many health professionals, including Doctor Coral Dixon. (General Practitioner /MBChB/BHB/ DipPaeds/ FRNZCGP). Dr Dixon adds that ...

"This area of health is still not given the attention and emphasis it deserves." Dr Dixon is one of the Family Doctors in Tauranga, New Zealand. She has affirmed that a large proportion of both psychological and physical illnesses are influenced by how individuals perceive and manage lifestyle stress. Doctor Dixon confirms that *"chronic stress is very well acknowledged to cause inappropriate and maladaptive chronic stress hormone responses, which can have wide-ranging effects on a huge number of organs and systems. Stress hormone elevation has both direct and indirect effects on many body organs and functions, and can be a significant contributor to a range of potentially serious health conditions. The critical link between psycho-social-physical (and spiritual) health has been recognised by many sophisticated cultures over many centuries and yet the typical modern lifestyle appears to have compromised overall health, by focusing primarily on physical health. It is imperative that individuals seeking optimal overall health recognise and value the importance of the mind-body connection, and understand that lifestyle choices are integral to health outcomes. Recognising, reducing and diffusing stress*

responses are undeniably a very important part of the quest for optimal health and happiness."

The issue of stress has been a problem for me for many years; it has affected my emotions, thinking ability, physical health and behaviour. So now when stress levels rise I begin to evaluate my emotions and look at things practically to help myself realistically gauge what is possible. This nearly always prevents stress from taking over and ruining my day.

Fear of Driving

I was afraid to drive a car and didn't get my license until I was twenty-eight years old and about to give birth to my first child. I had never heard of people being afraid of driving before, so was quite surprised to find out it was actually a fear shared by many others.

Other things that concerned me constantly were:
- Failing at school and work.
- Worrying about not having enough food or money made me a bit stingy at times.
- Powerlessness to protect my loved ones from having a serious accident or being diagnosed with a serious disease.
- My house being burgled or broken into.
- Encountering spiders and other insects such as cockroaches.
- Being forced to move away from the familiar or the pressure to change and do something in a different way.

My family would probably say, that I was rather over-protective, too sensitive, controlling and sometimes difficult. I would do most things for them because they wouldn't do it right, soon enough or well enough. I'm still working on that.

Looking back now, through my freedom spectacles, I would have done life quite differently if I was living without fear. I would have been bold enough to choose a career path that I now understand

I would have loved and would have been more than capable of doing. I would have approached parenting from a different angle and I would have been a better wife and mum. I do not think I was a bad mother but hindsight is great isn't it? I would have loved my family, friends and community more freely, would have been easier going and at peace. The good thing is that the grace of God is flowing and I also have a lot of time left to do some valuable things.

Pain Management Strategy

When fear rules we are in emotional pain and life is very hard. There are no pills for this kind of pain like there is for physical pain, but somehow desperation for survival kicks in and we create our very own pain management strategy.

Full of initiative, we come up with a string of behaviours that we think will deal with the pain when fear is rearing its ugly head. Let's compare painkillers with these behaviours. We take pain killers to cover up pain to provide relief while our body is healing. Painkillers are not the cure in themselves, we take them to numb the pain and help us get through a time of physical suffering of some kind. Many of us have frequent pains like headaches or muscle aches, we just down the painkillers and get on with our day. Using these pills extensively over a long period of time can have a detrimental effect on our health.

Fear produces emotional pain, so we adopt certain behaviours to help us deal with that pain and help us get through each day. The behaviours are not the cure in themselves, in fact they are detrimental to us long term, and actually do not help the situation short term, we just think they do. It is like we manufacture our own pills to take care of our fear, but in actual fact we make ourselves more sick. The behaviours are actually opening doors to more issues and these issues are good buddies with fear. You will find out more about these buddies in chapter three.

The good thing is, that God has organised peace for us through Jesus Christ, and that peace is on standby at all times for all who want or need it. During the hardest battles you can choose to apply the Word...

*Do not be anxious about anything,
but in every situation, by prayer and petition,
with thanksgiving, present your requests to God.
And the peace of God, which
transcends all understanding, will guard
your hearts and your minds in Christ Jesus.*
Philippians 4:6-7

Fear is the opposite of faith
Fear says you can't, it doesn't trust.
It hinders, weakens and debilitates.
Faith says you can, even when you cannot see or understand.
Faith trusts God. It allows, authorises and empowers.

---

*"If you can?" said Jesus.
"Everything is possible for one who believes."*
Mark 9:23

*Jesus said to the woman,
"Your faith has saved you; go in peace."*
Luke 7:50

> *And without faith it is impossible to please God, because anyone who comes to Him must believe that He exists and that He rewards those who earnestly seek Him.*
>
> Hebrews 11:6

After reading this chapter, do you have a lot more fear than you originally thought you had?

There is Hope
If you are struggling with fear or anxiety, there is hope; we just have a little work to do to get your mind into the right place. Fear ruled my life for a very long time, in fact decades, I did not realise that this was not normal. I had no idea that I didn't have to be like this, that I could be free.

There is most definitely hope for the fear enslaved captive. I have hounded heaven for freedom and I can tell you that God has and is answering my prayer.

> *God loves me for who I am,
> He can see deep inside.
> Nothing to prove and nothing to hide,
> me, He can see.*
>
> Janene Forlong 1981

Your Reflections

Chapter 2:
The Road to Fear

So how did you become fearful, which fork in the road did you veer off on to get to the place where fear rules? If we can work out how you journeyed to fear then we can discover how you can overcome and voyage out.

Fear isn't something you wanted or specifically chose; you allowed it in without realising and became captive. You are chained to the fear until you gain enough knowledge and understanding to empower you to overcome it.

The Good Life

We only get one chance at life and therefore we all generally desire that that one life should be a good one. The Bible tells us that Jesus came to give us abundant life, so we know that a rich and good life is what we were offered, but if we are fearful we will be unlikely to have any idea what a rich or abundant life could look like, let alone experience it.

> *The thief comes only to steal, kill and destroy;*
> *I have come that they may have life,*
> *and have it to the full.*
>
> John 10:10

So somehow you have had 'the good life' stolen from you, you let the thief in and he took your joy, your peace and your freedom. How did he gain the right to do that? This is a good question and one that deserves an answer.

'The good life' does not mean that nothing bad happens to you.

What it does mean is, that you can live life to the full, without fear, because you know that God is taking care of everything. Even when there are difficult things to deal with.

I am grateful that in most ways I had a very blessed childhood. I have four siblings, my parents are great people, and they loved us, parented us well and showed us how to love others. I went to good schools, was part of a wonderful church where I made some incredible lifelong friends. I even started my career working for a reputable company and had the best boss you could ask for in your first job. This boss helped me get my second job because he believed in me, I couldn't have asked for more.

However, there were lots of little things and one or two bigger ones, as I mentioned in the first chapter, that tripped my heart. They caused me to be fearful, doubt myself and become less confident about who I was. I became unsure about what I could achieve, if anything. So, fear can become a major thorn in almost anyone's life, you don't need to have gone through the worst ever experience or been born into the world's worst family, if there is such a thing.

Doors
The word 'doors' has been commonly used to communicate how we often give license to certain feelings and emotions in our lives, and in this case, it could be helpful to continue with that idea.

When you allow a negative thought time and space to run over and over in your mind, there is the potential that you will actually open a door in your mind and let that negative thought in to stay for good. If you then give that thought constant play, it becomes a familiar feeling and takes root in your emotions. You now have a new emotional habit in your thought patterns; a new piece of furniture, the big problem is that it will be impacting your belief system. This is how we begin to believe lies about ourselves; that is how fear takes root.

I've heard it said that it takes twenty-one days to create or break a habit, I'm not sure if that is always true but I am sure it is easier to start a habit than to stop one. The habit of fear happens so easily. As a comparison, say one day you smoke a cigarette, you haven't yet decided that you are going to be a smoker but you have one smoke. The next day you have two, the next day you have three and a number of days later you realise you enjoy smoking cigarettes, you keep on doing it. You are now creating a habit, but not only a habit, an addiction. We can create addictions with cigarettes, alcohol, sugar, caffeine, food, reactions, responses, moods, it's easy to do. It is equally easy to commence habitual thinking and ten times harder to break.

There are two different main doors that fear uses to gain access. Firstly, fear can be inherited and secondly it can enter through shocking or traumatic circumstances. As I mentioned in chapter one, for me it was a bit of both. It is important to unpack how fear entered and what doors it used, as this will help in the eviction process.

Words
Let's look at a scenario....

When I was ten, I was in a children's choir and asked to sing a solo. But on the day I froze and felt bad because I messed it up. This negative experience played frequently in my thought life from that time on.

As I got older, I heard people say negative things about my voice. One person said my singing voice sounded funny, and I overheard someone else say that their daughter's voice was better than mine.

In my teenage years, I was in a vocal group with three others and the group did really well with many opportunities to perform, and we won a lot of competitions. But I struggled to do the solos that were shared around the group and often opted out. I feared that my voice was not that good and must sound a little funny.

Having listened and believed what numerous people said, I allowed their opinions to determine the truth. Even though I really wanted to be a good soloist, I soon found it consistently difficult to sing in front of people.

What road led me to the belief that my singing voice was not very good? Listening to what others said and believing that what they said must be the truth. I now understand, that if I had chosen to run with my passion, without listening to what others said and had the singing lessons I needed, I may have turned out to be a good singer. I also understand now, that I was far too sensitive to other people's opinions; I opened the door to doubt, failure and fear. I altered the truth based upon what others said, that is very dangerous.

Sometimes the road to fear is words, words that are spoken often and repeatedly over time. When I was young there was a joke bandied around that I was dumb and stupid. It wasn't meant to harm or hurt anyone as it was done in humour, but unfortunately it went on for quite some years and the words went into my spirit and I believed them. I grew up believing that when the brains were dished out in our family, it was more generously given to the older siblings. I was obviously not going to accomplish much as I was not smart enough.

Bullying
Sometimes the road to fear is bullying. I would never want to down play the value of school, but we all know about the amount of bullying that takes place there amongst the students, and sometimes even the teachers. Bullying is a growing issue because of social media, but we are more aware of it now and much is being done to prevent it from happening.

When I was six I got my first pair of glasses. Back then, in 1970, spectacles were certainly not a fashion statement. Later on, when I was around thirteen, I got braces on my teeth as they were a real mess. I am so glad Mum and Dad paid that huge amount of money to fix them up. However, just prior to getting the braces my nickname, or mock-name, was Four Eyes. Once I had the braces put on, I was Tin Teeth and Four Eyes. This wasn't something that could be taken as a joke, seriously!

Trauma

Sometimes the road to fear is a traumatic event. A few years ago, my family and I were involved in a very serious and ugly car crash. Looking back, it is hard to believe that all four of us came out of it mostly unscathed, just a few minor injuries that we recovered from quickly. Our children were about ten and twelve years old at the time. It was a 'T' crash, we rammed into a vehicle driven by an elderly gentleman who had pulled out from a stop sign on the open road. The sad thing is the driver died a few days later and I understand his wife, who was in the passenger seat, deteriorated quickly afterwards but lived. She of course went through the trauma of the crash and then the horrific loss of her husband.

I had experienced some natural anxiety on the roads most of my life, but after this I was intensely fearful for about ten years. I didn't trust anyone sitting at a stop sign waiting to pull out, I feared each driver would make a wrong decision. The place where it happened is still a little nerve racking for me to drive through, but I have a lot less of a fear issue now.

I wrote earlier about the sexual abuse I experienced when I was six years old. I understand that this will be the number one trauma in my life and the one that set fear in motion.

I am writing these things in the hope that you will identify with at least some of them. Of course, there are people who have gone through harder things than I will ever know about. But what I do want to confirm is, without us needing pity, it is important to identify that these things had an impact on our life's journey. These things featured on our road to fear. We need to bring them up, talk about them and accept them as our past. We need to forgive and become whole again so we can move forward with a new sense of vitality, freedom and purpose.

How did you stray from the good life, what road took you to where fear rules?
- ❖ Was it words, bullying or trauma?
- ❖ What were the words that were spoken over you? Where did the words come from?
- ❖ Where were you bullied? How has that impacted you?
- ❖ What kind of trauma did you experience?

Bitter or better, fearful or free
When we are vulnerable, sick, grieving over a lost loved one, sexually abused, bullied, or a host of other traumatic situations, we can allow fear to enter our lives. We will not realise we are opening the door to this ugly and unhelpful emotion at the time.

There is the saying that 'we can become bitter or better', and in this case 'we can be fearful or free'. If you have already opened the door to fear there is hope, you can be free once more.

Your Reflections

Chapter 3:
Fear and Friends

When fear rules, don't be surprised if it hosts a party and invites some of its many friends. The door has already been flung wide open and now fear is settled in with its feet up. You may have hardly noticed all its friends starting to arrive, some of them have already moved in. If it is true that we become like those we spend time with, then we must be careful who we invite into our mind's home. Let's take a look at who some of these friends may be. Keep in mind there are a lot more friends than those I list here.

Shame

Let me tell you about Shame. Shame is shy, very present but a bit quiet during the party, if you know what I mean. There will be no fanfare or announcement when shame arrives. No, this friend will be unannounced and will choose to dance quietly in the corner.

We are often embarrassed and find it uncomfortable to admit that we are fearful of anything, because if we do, people will know that we are broken. So, to keep things looking perfect and well-maintained we manage, or even control our lifestyle so efficiently that no one guesses what is going on. Confessing that we are allowing our fears to rule our lives would never do!

I was really embarrassed and full of shame when I realised that I had a fear of germs, as I thought people would think I was a freak and needed help. I hated being where there was potentially a high level of unhygienic surfaces, products or even people. To be honest, I found it difficult to be comfortable anywhere. I was in quite a predicament and freedom from this would produce a great outcome, but I honestly couldn't see how that could ever happen, especially when I couldn't ask for help. I felt full of shame, hopeless and like a real failure.

Addiction

Addiction is the condition of being abnormally dependent or committed to a habit, practice or substance to the extent that its cessation causes trauma. Addiction is an excessively clingy and focused friend of fears. It fixates on one or more kinds of comfort and sets up a plan to make sure needs are met on an hourly or daily routine. Addiction's ability to keep this strict routine set in motion is incredible, in that it is willing to lie and steal at low or high levels in order to protect and provide for perceived needs.

I believe that fear can end up looking and behaving like an addiction, in how we become dependent or even committed to the fears that rule our lives. We are afraid to be free. I was afraid of intimacy, and though I did at times ask God to heal me and set me free from it, I was also scared he would answer the prayer and then I would have to do the very thing I was afraid of. I was only asking because I knew it was the right thing to do, but in all honesty, I didn't really mind if I was free or not. I was addicted and co-dependent on fear. While in captivity we forget how to live life freely and any notion to be free can be the most fearful thing of all because we are addicted to fear.

Control

Control calls the shots, demands, restrains, dominates and commands. Emotions are running high in the home when fears are being protected and preventions are being endorsed. Control can be quite a noisy friend of fear, although not always. It is the friend that pushes to get its own way, often uses lots of tears, is easily hurt and angered or impatient for fear of things being late or out of control. We create good coping mechanisms to control those around us so we don't have to confront our fear.

This friend called 'Control' will help you...

- ❖ Cover up fears, explain them away or even lie about them.
- ❖ Control situations to get their own way for fear of an unthinkable outcome.
- ❖ Train you up with good avoidance skills so you don't have to do what you fear.
- ❖ Have rigid opinions, be inflexible, unyielding, unreasonable, or unable to take others' opinions or outlooks on-board. It's my way or the highway!
- ❖ Use past experiences to control future outcomes.
- ❖ Be aware that others find you difficult, but help you stay in denial as to the reason why.

I am aware now that I controlled situations, particularly at home, so that I could be sure that the outcomes would be what I wanted or needed them to be. I wasn't very flexible or easy to please. I definitely used past experiences to control decision making, and I mean in an 'over the top' kind of way. I didn't trust that the past would stay in the past; I feared it would always repeat itself no matter what.

Jealousy

To be jealous is to covet, be envious or have a grudging admiration and desire to have something that is possessed by another. Jealousy is a bit of a sly friend of fear, it is not overly obvious, though can produce outbursts when the emotional pain is at a high level.

Jealousy comes in when we are feeling like a failure, unworthy, rejected, offended or unforgiving. We desire the opportunities, experiences or achievements that we see in others and we start to think and believe that 'it's just not fair.'

Jealousy has a really close friend called 'Self Pity' who cannot see why they of all people should be in the situation they are in. There is a lot of pain carried inside this friend and things can get a bit ugly at times.

*Anger is cruel and fury overwhelming,
but who can stand before jealousy?*
Proverbs 27:4

*For where you have envy and selfish ambition,
there you find disorder and every evil practice.*
James 3:16

When you are fearful it is really difficult not to allow jealousy in; after all, a fear captive is not experiencing a rich and abundant life. For years I coveted a friend's ministry, which now seems so ridiculous, but at the time I couldn't understand why I seemed to be going nowhere and they were experiencing the height of success so early in life.

Unforgiveness
One of Fear's very moody friends is 'Unforgiving.' It comes with behavioural difficulties like taking offence, holding grudges, having little to no mercy and harshness that is a bit cutting at times.

Taking offence is a terrible thing and a very difficult habit to abandon. You often read no action, acknowledgment or response as rejection. You take it hard. You may be unable to determine or focus on the fact that your friends and family love you and would have good motive, you may even believe the worst in every situation. If you have been previously wounded in your spirit you are already in pain so you have no 'defence' to the 'offence.'

As you can understand, unforgiveness is much harder on the person who is finding it hard to forgive. Often the one who has done the wrong is completely unaware. The bible gives us very good motivation to forgive:

> *"And when you stand praying,
> if you hold anything against anyone,
> forgive them, so that your Father in heaven
> may forgive you your sins."*
> Mark 11:25

Small mindedness

I wouldn't be at all surprised if Fears 'best friend' is Small-Mindedness. To be small-minded means to have a narrow or selfish attitude, to be petty, ungenerous and mean spirited. This small-minded friend of fear is often negative and anxious about how things will work out.

It makes sense to me, that once fear is ruling the roost, the shutters have closed and the view has narrowed extensively. Being small-minded is the best way to keep things safe, predictable and to prevent possible hazards. The biggest thing it will put a stop to is change: it makes you believe change is dangerous and things must remain as they are, by hook or by crook! Once this friend has had home set up for a while, it becomes familiar and anything outside of familiar is unsafe, unpredictable and dangerous. So, in the mind of the fearful, it is a jolly good friend!

People are not always selfish because they want to be, they're not necessarily stingy because they don't want to be generous. It is a vicious circle; they want to be who they really are, but because of fear, they are unable to be broad-minded as that would surely mean they are unprotected and insecure. They may even hate that they are like that but do not know how to be who they really are.

Poor-spirited

Fear has a significant but understated friend called Poor-Spirited. This is a friend you could almost feel sorry for, but they will need to be evicted. It arrives lacking courage and won't fight you for anything as it is too timid and cowardly.

One day, just in the past few years, God spoke to me and said "You are poor spirited." I didn't like what I heard, but I knew at once that it was true and that it determined how I felt about myself, my thought patterns, decision making and the choices I made. I even seemed to have this underlying belief that I had little or no worth and I didn't deserve to be blessed. This is not true, of course; the devil had sold this lie to me a long time ago and I bought it.

To be honest, fear strips us of all our potential, especially our courage, strength and resolution. As it strips us of the qualities we need to succeed in reaching our destiny, it exchanges them for the things that undermine us and cause us to feel inadequate and hopeless.

I know that I went through a lot of years lacking courage, but God has healed me and given me back that courage. The journey I have been on has strengthened me to the point where I have more courage than ever before. I believe that it is true that God turns all things for good to those that love Him, just as it says in His Word.

Unbelief

Unbelief is an unbelievably difficult friend to deal with, pardon the pun. This friend doesn't make a big entrance, it crawls in quietly. But there will be an underlying, strong presence of unbelief that will be firmly felt and this can alter the tones of the personality and character of the person.

It is really important to believe that the good things we experience in life come from the father of all good gifts, God. We cannot have a relationship with God if we do not believe in Him and believe that He is who He says He is.

Life can be quite unbearable while struggling with unbelief, as this friend puts a major halt on almost anything that holds hope in high esteem. We need to believe in ourselves, our children, our loved ones and our friends. How about vision and passion and ideas?

Unbelief impacts the trust element in relationships, interferes with the decision-making process and expects things to fail. What strength do we have when we don't believe?

Unbelief is mentioned many times in the bible, as it is the opposite of faith. It also mentions in Hebrews chapter 3, that unbelief is an outright sin. The Israelites were unable to enter God's rest because of their unbelief. We can see in Psalm 106:24-25 that where there is unbelief there can also be grumbling, complaining and discontent.

Impatience
If we are lacking in patience, we are unwilling to wait for something or someone. We are often restless, short tempered, easily irritated and lacking in tolerance. We will find delays or opposition very trying. Impatient people are often very uncomfortable people to be around, as stress and impatience are good friends, although not a good combo at all.

Oh dear, I have known this friend far too well. I was given a word of knowledge when I was twenty-one about this very thing. I was in a room with around thirty other young people; we were about to tour New Zealand together using music, dance and drama to present a great message of love and hope. I was really looking forward to receiving an encouraging personal word from the lovely gentleman. He went around the entire group prophesying and when he got to me he said "You are impatient." Wow, that hit me really hard, I didn't like that. Why would God want to say that to me and not something nice? Anyway, it was true and I have been working on it ever since, it's a hard one to evict.

> *We do not want you to become lazy, but to imitate those who through faith and patience inherit what has been promised.*
> Hebrews 6:12

Anger

Anger is a strong feeling of displeasure and antagonism aroused by a real or supposed wrong.

Here is a noisy and highly emotional friend of Fear. If you do not want to connect with 'Anger' too often then I suggest you make sure things don't go wrong, are not delayed or hindered. If things do go wrong, then one of Anger's best mates, 'Blame Shifting,' may kick into action with the knowledge of how and when everything went so terribly wrong. Of course, there will certainly be someone to charge with the responsibility. The interesting thing is that once all the drama has finished, everyone feels a whole lot worse than they did before. The moral of the story being that neither 'Anger' nor 'Blame Shifting' achieved anything of any value.

> *"In your anger do not sin":*
> *Do not let the sun go down*

*while you are still angry,
and do not give the devil a foothold.*
Ephesians 4: 26, 27

Self-seeking
Self-seeking is the act or practice of selfishly advancing one's own ends. This narrow-focused friend surely opposes love, making it difficult for us to choose to put others first.

When life is as potentially dangerous as one may fear, it is easy to allow this friend in for a long stay. Out of fear we become overly interested in getting our own way, often not noticing how this affects others and missing what our loved ones need or want. We adopt behavioural patterns that make sure the ball is always in our court, and somehow we manage to delude ourselves into thinking that what we are doing is perfectly okay.

Confusion
Confusion comes in like a flood when there are numerous fears. There will be a lack of clarity, certainty and the captive is unable to work things through to a good outcome or clear understanding. When fear has ruled for a long-time, confusion is considered normal, it is now one of the familiar close friends.

The confused captive is often unable to see that they have any problems or need help. They may not understand they are missing out on a rich and abundant life or how they could take hold of what is on offer.

Fear changes people for the worse, by stripping us of our confidence and making us vulnerable to the attacks of our enemy, Satan. What was once truth is now lies and what was knowledge is no longer the understanding that we live our lives by. We have no protection over our minds and emotions. What used to be good reason is now blurred severely with confusion.

There are many other 'Friends of Fear' that I have not talked about here, such as 'Complaining', 'Grumbling,' 'Bitterness,' and 'Slander.' All of who ruin our lives, upset our loved ones and lead us away from the abundant life God has destined for us. I had to specifically target the area of complaining in my life, as it was a well-entrenched friend. It is so much more enjoyable looking on the bright side and dealing with issues in a calm manner.

With friends on board, the party is now in full swing and the issue is much bigger and more complicated for the fear enslaved captive. They are no longer the person they once were, were meant to be, or wanted to be.

To be honest, just thinking about all this is confusing. That is how it is with fear and a party of friends that don't just come for the evening, but move in to stay forever, unless you set the eviction date!

Getting rid of unwanted friends

Later in the book we will look at how to evict the friends we do not want and definitely do not need. It is important to remember, when we are evicting, that we need to name each one and deal with them individually. Although they network together they do have different roots.

After the eviction, the best thing to do is to thoughtfully kick-start some new healthy habits to take the place of the old behaviours, or 'friends of fear' as we have called them. You will find chapter six a helpful tool for this.

- ❖ Do you agree that we invite bad behaviours into the house of our mind to protect our fears?
- ❖ Which of these friends is your fear friends with?

❖ Are there any others that have not been mentioned?

Write the friends of your fears into this prayer and pray it out loud.

PRAYER: Father, forgive me for being ....

....

....

Thank you for your forgiveness, help me to overcome my fear your way, with your help. In Jesus name, amen.

Your Reflections

Chapter 4:

What the Bible Says

It is important to know what the bible says about fear, as this will help us re-claim the correct perspective. Fear warps our mindset, but God's Word can adjust and restore it.

We all have default thought patterns, responses and actions. For example: if the default font on a computer is Calibri and we do not work out how to change the default font, we will have to manually change it each time we create a new document. You keep getting what you've got unless you proactively make the change. You can choose to change your thought patterns from negative to positive. You can choose to put a stop to the record playing thoughts going on in your head, that lead you down the destructive path of fear.

The Bible mentions fear a lot, in fact there are 365 mentions of 'Fear not' or 'Do not be afraid.' That is clearly one for every day of the year. God knows we face fear and anxiety, it is often a daily battle and evidently we need the encouragement.

God didn't give us fear

> *...for God has not given us the spirit of fear; but of power, and of love, and of a sound mind.*
> 2 Timothy 1:7

Notice that this scripture uses the words, 'spirit of fear.' We don't like to call all the issues we face, 'a spirit,' but the Bible clearly states here that that this is what fear is. Most translations of this verse use the word 'spirit.' If it is a spirit, then we need to treat it like a spirit. We will deal with this appropriately in chapter six.

It was never God's intention for us to battle fear. What He did plan for us is power, love and a sound mind. If these three things were constant for us, life would be a whole lot more pleasant and meaningful. In the message translation, it says: 'God doesn't want us to be shy with His gifts, but bold and loving and sensible.' Imagine that, what would your life be like if you were experiencing power, love and a sound mind at all times?

Power
If we are wisely wielding the power that Jesus has given us, then we can deal with anything that comes against us in His name. It doesn't matter if it is physical, emotional, spiritual or mental, Jesus' power works on all fronts.

- ❖ If you could live without fear and walk in the power God has given you, what would your life look like?
- ❖ How would that be different to now?

Sound Mind
With a sound mind we have the freedom and ability to make good and right judgements.

The message translation of this verse calls these three things that God gives us, 'gifts.' I love receiving gifts, don't you? Isn't it fun when gifts arrive surprisingly by courier? You rush to the door to see who the package is for. "Oh it's for me," you say excitedly. "Ooo I wonder what it is?" Your voice is rising with expectation. You open the beautifully package gift and your heart sinks. God sent you the gift of a sound mind, sometimes call self-discipline! "Oh how boring," you say.

Now, take a moment to think about what this gift could mean if you opened it and used it. Constant peace, self-control, no stress or anxiety. Life would be much more of a breeze than it ever has been before. Not such a bad gift after all, is it? In fact it has far more value than most gifts we get, right?

- ❖ What would your life look like if you had a sound mind, constantly?
- ❖ How would that be different to now?

I can do all things through Him Who strengthens me.
Philippians 4:13

Perfect love casts out fear

If we allow God's perfect love to penetrate right through our spirit, we will not be afraid because His perfect love casts out fear.

There is no fear in love; but perfect love casts out fear, because fear involves punishment, and the one who fears is not perfected in love. We love, because He first loved us.
1 John 4:18-19

- ❖ How can God's love help you with your fear?
- ❖ Are you afraid of punishment? Why?
- ❖ What can you do to be perfected in God's love?

I love the fact that God didn't give us fear, He knows we struggle with it and has made a way for us to be free. It says in the scripture above: 'The one who fears is not perfected in love.' We all have so much to learn about God's love, and the longer we are on this journey of discovering 'who' God essentially is, the more His love will be flooding through our being. His love will diminish our fear. I believe fear and perfect love cannot exist together, the answer to freedom lies in a deep genuine love relationship with God Himself.

Fear opposes faith

If fear is a state of unpleasant or disturbing feelings induced by perceived danger, and faith is the confidence in what we hope for and assurance about what we do not see [Hebrews 11:1], then it seems to me that faith opposes fear. Let's take a look at how the Bible shows us that faith and fear are unable to co-exist:

Fear	Faith	Bible
Unable to please God	Pleases God	Hebrews 11:6 ...without faith it is impossible to please God.
Is anxious and has no peace	Casts anxiety on God and finds peace	Philippians 4:6-7 Do not be anxious.... present your requests ... and the peace of God will guard your hearts...
Downcast Disturbed	Puts hope in God and praises Him	Psalm 42:5 Why, my soul, are you downcast? ... Put your hope in God, for I will yet praise Him, my Saviour and my God.
Is weak	Achieves all things with Jesus' strength	Philippians 4:13 I can do all things through Him who strengthens me.
Doubts	Believes that God exists	Hebrews 11:6 ...anyone who comes to Him must believe that He exists and that He rewards those who earnestly seek Him.
Worries about life	Trusts God to provide	Luke 12:22 ...Do not worry about your life, what you will eat: or about your body, what you will wear.

Afraid to be alone	Is never alone, God is their helper	Hebrews 13:5-6 … "Never will I leave you; never will I forsake you." So, we say with confidence, "The Lord is my helper; I will not be afraid....
Captive to fear	Delivered from fear	Philippians 4:19 I sought the Lord and He answered me. He delivered me from all my fears.
Overcome by evil	Fights the evil one and overcomes	Ephesians 6:16 … take up the shield of faith, with which you can extinguish all the flaming arrows of the evil one.

Fear impacted my faith severely, but the more freedom I gained the more my faith strengthened. The journey toward freedom from fear started when I decided to fully put my trust in God, even though I really wasn't sure He would come through for me. I just decided there was nothing or no one else who could help me. If God didn't or wouldn't, I was a hopeless case. He came through for me and because of that I know for sure that He delivers us from all fear, and of course it says so in His Word.

I sought the Lord and He answered me,
He delivered me from all my fears.
Psalm 34:4

❖ Is your fear impacting your trust and belief in God?
❖ Are you worried about your life? What and why?
❖ Which verses in the chart encourage you the most and why?

If you are living with fear you may struggle with doubt and unbelief. But you can choose to wield your weapon of faith [Ephesians 6:16] to shield yourself from the enemies' flaming arrows of things like doubt and unbelief. Do that a few times and you will see your faith start building and strengthening as you begin to win. Remember we only need a small amount of faith to achieve anything.

> The Apostles said to the Lord, "Increase our faith!" And the Lord said, "If you had faith like a mustard seed, you would say to this mulberry tree, 'Be uprooted and be planted in the sea'; and it would obey you."
>
> Luke 17:5, 6

In Hebrews 11 we see that many people chose to trust in God and put their faith in Him. They decided that the heavenly kingdom was worth more than all they had here in this temporary life. They gave their lives to obey and trust God, allowing Him to save them from physical danger, to provide food, clothing and shelter and to deliver them from their enemies.

Hebrews 11:32-38 reads:

And what shall I say? I do not have time to tell you about Gideon, Barak, Samson and Jephthah, about David and Samuel and the prophets, who through faith conquered kingdoms, administered justice, and gained what was promised; who shut the mouths of lions, quenched the fury of the flames, and escaped the edge of the sword; whose weakness was turned to strength; and who became powerful in battle and routed foreign armies. Women received back their dead, raised to life again. There were others who were tortured, refusing to be released so that they might gain an even better resurrection. Some faced jeers and flogging, and even chains and imprisonment. They were put to death by stoning; they were sawed in two; they were killed by the sword. They went about in sheepskins and goatskins, destitute, persecuted and mistreated— the world was not worthy of them. They wandered in deserts and mountains, living in caves and in holes in the ground.

I find these scriptures very encouraging. They show us we are not alone in our struggles and have very real reasons to be afraid at times. We certainly are not wimps but we are vulnerable to the evil actions of the enemy. Life is often tough for us all but we can choose to rise up above the fear and conquer as those before us did. We will look at how to do this more specifically later in this book.

- ❖ Which characters do you find most inspiring, and why?
- ❖ What would you like written about you in the future, so others can be inspired?

Jesus was here on earth for thirty-three years and He experienced temptation, rejection, grief, hatred, scorn, conflict, betrayal and of course the awful events that led Him to the cross. He knows the terrible pain that we go through, He understands it all. We must know that because of what Jesus did on the cross, we are able to live life, suffer as He did, but with the strength and victory that He purchased for us. We can face difficulties with courage to overcome, just as He did on the cross.

It is important to strengthen our faith, especially if we want to evict fear. We can do this by reading God's Word. The bonus is that when we begin to have the victory over just one little fear, our faith will automatically be strengthened.

God wants us to trust Him like a little child trusts a father. Our Heavenly Father wants us to let Him provide for us, care for us and help us. He wants us to call out to Him and tell Him what we need. He is a huge God, very capable and He has been a father for a very long time. When we are overly independent, and dare I say it, a bit controlling at times, we can prevent Him from helping us.

There is a team building exercise where one person stands on the stage with their back to two lines of people who have arms outstretched ready to catch their team mate. The person on the stage, must then fall backwards into the arms of their teammates, trusting they will catch them and not let them fall to the floor. The question is, do we trust God to catch us when we fall?

Do you believe God will catch you, deliver you, help you and provide for your every need?

Let's remind ourselves of these verses once again…

> *Cast your cares on the Lord*
> *and He will sustain you:*
> *He will never let the*
> *righteous be shaken.*
> Psalm 55:22

*Trust in the lord
with all your heart
and lean not on your understanding;
in all your ways
submit to Him
and He will make your paths straight.*
Proverbs 3:5, 6

Chapter 5:

Why Choose Freedom?

Fear not, for I have redeemed you;
I have summoned you by name; you are mine.
Isaiah 43:1

Why choose freedom? Or should I ask why choose fear? That is probably a more important question to ask. In the verse above we are told not to fear, and as I have said before, 'do not be afraid' or 'fear not' is mentioned at least 365 times in the Bible. Why wouldn't anyone want to be free from fear?

The thing is that generally those of us who live with fear have forgotten what freedom is, we cannot remember as it has been far too familiar for far too long. We have become co-dependent on fear itself. It is all we know and there are no surprises. We may say: "At least we know what we are up against, it is safe."

I know how embarrassing and shameful it feels to admit that we are fearful. It is easier to continue to surrender to the fear and proudly fight on to keep things the way they are, because the transition will be too uncomfortable.

All over the world people are fighting for all kinds of freedom; many groups and individuals are standing up for racial freedom, just remuneration, gender equality and freedom of speech. Tremendous work is being done to fight human trafficking and many other forms of slavery, which is rampant across the globe. Much of this is very important, in that it is rescuing the masses who have lived and breathed suffering most of their lives.

We have been rescued and gifted a liberty that has already been bought and paid for by Jesus Christ. We are presented with a rich and abundant life. Fighting for freedom of any kind, is not easy, battles never are. But becoming 'who' you have been created to be is something worth the time it takes. God will be with you every step of the way as He wants you to be free too.

> *So do not fear, for I am with you;*
> *do not be dismayed, for I am your God.*
> *I will strengthen you and help you;*
> *I will uphold you with my righteous right hand.*
> Isaiah 41:10

God did not plan for us to be fearful

I can remember wishing I had more courage to do the things I really wanted to do, and that I wouldn't be so afraid of people or what might happen to me. I imagine that most fear enslaved persons greatly desire to be people who have power, love and to be calm with a sound mind. For those without this kind of peace and strength it is the greatest and most valuable gift. If it is true that God did not give us a fearful spirit, then we are right to realise fear is not meant for us, and we can ask God for what He did give, the power, the love and the sound mind.

> *For God did not give us a spirit of timidity*
> *(Of cowardice, of craven and cringing and fawning*
> *fear), but He has given us a spirit of power and of*
> *love and of calm and well-balanced mind and*
> *discipline and self-control.*
> 2 Timothy 1:7 AMP

You were called to be free

So, you are no longer a slave, but God's child;
and since you are His child,
God has made you also an heir.
Galatians 4:7

I encourage you to choose to fight fear and exchange it for liberty because you were called to freedom. We were not born to be slaves to anything, especially not fear. We are the children of the one and only God. It says in the first scripture in this chapter, God has called us by name and we are individually important to Him.

You, my brothers and sisters, were called to be free…
Galatians 5:13

We were predestined by God and therefore we have providence for this life and an inheritance awaiting us in heaven. We can rest in the knowledge that we did not arrive here by chance, God thought of us, designed us and created us. We can also rest in the promise that God has good plans for us, an enjoyable destiny that will prosper and provide us with a hope and a future.

"For I know the plans I have for you,"
declares the Lord,
"plans to prosper you and not to harm you,
plans to give you hope and a future."
Jeremiah 29:11

God's Promises
A life of freedom is a rich life packed with God's promises. Do your fears offer you protection, rest, peace, power, security, provision, eternal life, abundant life, freedom, love or comfort? God's promises offer us all we will ever need and so much more. For example:

- If we search for Him we will find Him - Deuteronomy 4:29
- He is near us - Deuteronomy 4:7
- Protection - Psalms 121
- His love will never fail - 1 Chronicles 16:34
- Blessing - Psalms 1:1–3 Ephesians 1:3
- Salvation - Romans 1:16–17
- All things will work out for good - Romans 8:28
- Comfort - 2 Corinthians 1:3–4
- A new life in Christ - 2 Corinthians 5:17
- He will finish the work He started - Philippians 1:6
- Peace - Philippians 4:6–7
- Provision - Matthew 6:33, Philippians 4:19, Matthew 6:26
- Rest - Matthew 11:28–30
- Abundant Life - John 10:10
- Eternal life - John 4:14
- Security - John 10:28
- Power - Acts 1:8

Ask yourself this question…
- What reasons do you have to choose freedom over fear?

What does Freedom look like?
Freedom is the condition of not being enslaved, restrained or held captive by anyone or anything. It is having the liberty to act and choose without control, or interference by a person, establishment or circumstance.

From my experience, freedom, after captivity, is like looking at life through a brand-new pair of perfectly prescribed glasses. Life through these glasses is beautiful and you can see it all in intricate detail just the way it should be. The unrealistic expectations, pressure, strain and tension are mostly gone; you can relax and enjoy each individual moment. You will re-learn how to rest, take in the view and smell the roses.

Moving away from the metaphorical, you will deal with issues more calmly and easily, in fact difficulties will appear smaller and less overwhelming. When you take a vacation you will know how to slow down and take it easy, allowing yourself to be effectively refreshed.

When your volume of work is building you will manage it more effectively and with little to no stress. You will realistically understand and appreciate the range of choices that are in front of you on a daily and long-term basis and feel free to choose with no restraint. Your world view will be a lot bigger possibly even global sized!

My Freedom Definition

After captivity, freedom is the right to full access to life as given and promised by God Himself, the perfect design for us to have abundant life.

This does not mean, however, that we can waste our lives or use it to hurt ourselves or others but we are supposed to fully live, be fully alive and make the most of this one life we have. In the final chapter of this book, we talk about the responsibility we have with our given freedom, this has nothing to do with rules but rather wisdom and power.

In the next chapter we look at 'how' you can fight to become free, but this chapter is all about 'why' you should choose to fight. It is important that you choose because the battle needs focus, time, commitment and passion. It is not a decision you make lightly. More than that, you need to trust God and have faith in Him, because the only way you are going to win this battle is by partnering with Him. It is His power you need and want. Just as the verse below says..." For when I am weak, then I am strong." If you, in your weakness give yourself to God, who is strong, He will be the strength you need to win the battle.

> *But He said to me, "My grace is sufficient for you, for my power is made perfect in weakness." Therefore, I will boast all the more gladly about my weaknesses, so that Christ's power may rest on me. That is why, for Christ's sake, I delight in weaknesses, in insults, in hardships, in persecutions, in difficulties. For when I am weak, then I am strong.*
>
> 2 Corinthians 12: 9,10

Biblical Cases

In the Bible we can read about many people who not only fought their own fear but were used by God to battle for the freedom of whole nations. Esther, Moses and David are three great examples:

Queen Esther battled to save the Jews from being eliminated during the reign of King Xerxes, and stared fear in the face as her very own life hung in the balance. The risk was extremely high with this being an era when a queen should never approach the king without first being summoned. This King was also unaware that Esther was a Jew. With encouragement from her cousin Mordecai, Esther approached the King informing him of her ancestry and revealed Haman's plan to kill her people. Esther had no idea how the King would take this information, but she had the favour of God upon her. This favour and anointing meant that the enemies plans were foiled and Esther and her people were saved.

Moses did not believe himself to be a gifted speaker let alone a lawyer or politician. He had made many serious moral mistakes as a young man, but God chose to use him to bring freedom for the Israelites. They had been slaves in Egypt for many years. Moses feared for his life each time he fronted up to Pharaoh with the words God gave him to speak, during the long and nasty verbal combat. It seemed like Pharaoh would never agree to let the people go, but after a multitude of heaven-sent horrid plagues, Pharaoh gave in. The Israelites finally left Egypt with the apparently ungifted Moses as their divinely appointed leader.

David fought and killed lions and bears while protecting his father's sheep, but surely confronting a giant Philistine was going to be another thing, or was it? The entire Israelite army were paranoid with fear, and not one of them would step out to fight Goliath in order to save the day. David believed God would be with him. The armour was too big and heavy, so he went out to battle the giant with a sling and a few stones from the stream. Goliath was killed by a kid who trusted God to win the battle for him, and it happened according to his faith.

From these biblical stories, we can glean that no matter what fears we face, we can win because God is with us.

- ❖ Do you identify with Queen Esther, Moses or David? How?
- ❖ What reasons do you have to choose freedom over fear?

Our fears may be giant sized
with Pharaoh sized tactics or
with things heavily stacked up against us,
as it was for Esther.

Battling fear is like facing a lion or a bear.
David learnt to face his fears when he was very
young and quite alone, but in these times he
discovered God was with him.

When you choose freedom, you will enter into battle but God is with you. You will overcome and afterwards you will have a powerful anointing just as David did. This was clearly showcased when he walked out courageously to fight the giant and overcame.

Your flight to freedom will begin when you make a definite choice of freedom over fear. Are you ready?

Chapter 6:

Flight to Freedom

When I was about thirteen years old, my Aunty Liz gave me a Bible around the time I chose to be baptised. She wrote a little note in the front of it and it included this verse that has become very special to me.

> *...being confident of this,*
> *that He who began a good work in you*
> *will carry it on to completion*
> *until the day of Christ Jesus.*
> Philippians 1:6

This verse is dearer to me now than ever before because I can actually see the hand of God working in my life, accomplishing deep things within me that I cannot achieve alone, making changes that I cannot make by myself. I am so grateful for the work He is doing and I ask Him to work all the more as I can see the value of what He has already done. I am now much more secure and at peace as a whole person.

We do not need to be afraid of God or the work He wants to do in our lives. He only does the work if we are willing. It is as we yield and say 'yes' to Him that He completes these good things. He has our best in mind; He wants us to be free, healed and whole. I can assure you that you will not be disappointed at what He will achieve in you, if you just have the courage to allow Him to bring out the best in you.

My heart feels very burdened when I see people bound up by fear. I know for certain that no one needs to be held captive like that. It is God's good and perfect will for us all to be free.

Once we gain the revelation that we can be free, we are able to journey to a point where we hate that which is binding us and holding us back. We must arrive here, at this place where we no longer want to be slaves to fear, because if we are happy to stay with the familiar we will not find our freedom. I guess you could say it is like taking a leap of faith in being willing to let God help us. I cannot promise it won't be painful, in fact I know it will be to start with, but I can promise it will be worth it!

The steps in this chapter are the direction my journey to freedom took. My prayer and hope is that this will be an encouragement to you to step forward in faith towards your freedom. This is a tool not a formula. It is more about you showing God that you are willing to trust Him on this journey. He will honour that choice and He loves to bring about healing and deliverance, so we know He is for us and not against us.

Using this tool will assist you to focus on the word of God to renew your mind, change how you think and encourage you to renew your self-talk. You will gain revelation that will, in time, bring about the freedom you have been longing for.

1. Choose Freedom

The first thing to do is to have the conversation with God telling Him you want to be free. He will obviously be delighted about this as you have now given Him the permission to work on your behalf. He will get onto it immediately, and remember, you cannot get free without Him. It is a spiritual battle and He is the one who will bring it about. Your job is to be willing to let God do the work.

For our struggle is not against flesh and blood,

> *but against the rulers, against the authorities,*
> *against the powers of this dark world*
> *and against the spiritual forces*
> *of evil in the heavenly realms.*
>
> Ephesians 6:12

It was sometime in 1986 that I wrote the song 'Flight to Freedom', this is the chorus:

> *My flight to freedom from the things*
> *that enslaved me, is beginning right now,*
> *thank God you saved me.*
> *I've chosen to fight; I know we will win.*
> *The end is in sight while I trust in Him.*

In the only way I knew how, I told God, way back then, that I wanted freedom. It has taken a long time, but I'm writing to say that He has freed me and continues to on a daily basis.

God wants you to be free too, and He will be with you on this journey in the easy times and the tough times. He has promised to complete His work. Do you desire to be completely free from fear?

Choosing to battle fear to gain your promised freedom can be a bit scary at times, but well worth it!. Just keep your eye on the goal and the one who paid for your freedom, Jesus. It is time to break out of your fear jail!

Pray this out loud, telling God you want freedom from fear. Let Him know you are willing to work with Him to evict your fears.

PRAYER: Lord, I understand that you did not give me the spirit of fear, but you did give me love, power and a sound mind. Please expose my fears to me, help me to evict them, and to take back the love, power and sound mind that you have given me. In Jesus name, amen.

2. Believe in the Name of Jesus

I sought the Lord, and He answered me:
He delivered me from all my fears.
Psalm 34:4

'Believing' is extremely important because you are putting your trust in the most powerful being, God. Through your belief you gain access to all of who He is, including His wisdom and His protection. Belief is gifted to you as an incredibly effective and powerful weapon that you have the right to use.

As you pray, while renouncing and evicting your fear, you may not specifically feel anything. Sometimes you do and sometimes you don't. If you don't, it does not mean nothing has happened. The best thing to do is to pray fervently and believe that God is doing what only He can do. You can take some encouragement from this excerpt from Mark 9:

'...When the spirit saw Jesus, it immediately threw the boy into a convulsion. He fell to the ground and rolled around, foaming at the mouth. Jesus asked the boy's father, "How long has he been like this?" "From childhood," he answered. "It has often thrown him into fire or water to kill him. But if you can do anything, take pity on us and help us." "'If you can'?" said Jesus. **"Everything**

*is possible for one who believes." Immediately the boy's father exclaimed, **"I do believe; help me overcome my unbelief!"***

When Jesus saw that a crowd was running to the scene, he rebuked the impure spirit. "You deaf and mute spirit," he said, "I command you, come out of him and never enter him again. "The spirit shrieked, convulsed him violently and came out. The boy looked so much like a corpse that many said, "He's dead." But Jesus took him by the hand and lifted him to his feet, and he stood up.'

Mark 9: 20-27

We must always believe and pray in Jesus' name; it is Jesus' name plus our faith in Him that makes the difference.

> *By faith in the name of Jesus, this man whom you see and know was made strong. It is Jesus' name and the faith that comes through Him that has completely healed him, as you can see.*

Acts 3:16

It is very important to believe that God will help you. He loves it when you trust Him and He is very capable of handling this battle you are fighting. It is also good to recognise that our faith is a very powerful tool in our weapon kit. If believing in Jesus' name secures us eternal life, I am sure that our faith and trust in God can help us evict our fear.

❖ Are you able to believe that God will help you in your freedom from fear journey?

3. Confess your fears

Now it is time to confess the fears that you know you have. In time you may realise you have a few more, but let's deal with the ones you know about for now.

Therefore, confess your sins to each other and pray for each other so that you may be healed. The prayer of a righteous person is powerful and effective

James 5:16

You have chosen freedom, now I believe it is really important to confess your fears, name them to God and admit them to yourself. We are often in denial about what we fear, and you cannot be free of something you are not prepared to admit to yourself, God or anyone else.

Because we have allowed a spirit of fear to rule our lives we haven't trusted God and believed in Him. Without faith we cannot please Him, so I confessed my fear as sin and I encourage you to do the same. It will be a huge weight off your shoulders when you have been honest with yourself and with God. It is always hard to start with but once you have started it will get easier.

It can be good to do this with a trusted friend who can bring discernment or counsel to the situation, also helping you discover how fear may have entered in the first place. Follow these steps:

- ❖ Write down the fears you are aware of in your life [page 22]
- ❖ How have these fears been affecting your life?
- ❖ Name the fears, call them what they are, e.g., 'Lies of the enemy'.

❖ Pray and renounce [give up] unbelief and each individual fear out loud. Evict the unbelief and fears by commanding them to leave in Jesus' name.

PRAYER:
I renounce and resist the spirit of unbelief, in the name of Jesus. I have decided that there is no longer a place in my mind, my heart or my life for unbelief and therefore I evict and command it to leave right now, through the mighty power of Jesus name, amen.

PRAYER:
I renounce and resist the spirit of fear, in the name of Jesus. I have decided that there is no longer a place in my mind, my heart or my life for any fear to rule my life. Therefore, I evict and command the fear of..

....

to leave right now, through the mighty power of Jesus name, amen.

4. Identify wrong behaviours

After you have prayed and evicted fear, it is time to focus on the behavioural patterns you have introduced to protect your fears. Remember in chapter 3, we talked about fear moving in, setting up house and inviting all its friends around for a housewarming party? These friends are bad habits and behaviours like control, selfishness, manipulation, taking offence, jealousy, pride, anger, boasting, selfishness, greed, unforgiveness and others. Fear of failure may be good friends with rejection and the fear of germs could be good friends with anger and shame.

❖ We may fear we won't have enough money or food so we become selfish, stingy, controlling or greedy

- ❖ We may struggle with the fear of rejection because we were adopted or didn't feel fully loved by our parents. This can cause us to be easily offended or struggle with jealousy.
- ❖ You may have been so hurt by someone that you are struggling to forgive them.
- ❖ Often our fear is so intense we think we are losing control. We may fear we're not going to make our deadline, or that things won't go the way we want them too, so we become impatient or develop a habit of being easily angered.

The important thing is to work out which behaviours you have adopted to assist you with your fear. We tend to make excuses for the way we behave, giving ourselves permission, but this is not right. It is time to man or woman-up! It's time to play spiritual detective with the Holy Spirit. Ask Him to help you identify these wrong behaviours. Be willing to hear what they are, write them down, confess them and ask God to help you to change your ways. Then you can begin to introduce new positive behaviours, such as forgiveness and patience, to assist you in your freedom.

Write down the wrong behaviours you have adopted because of fear. Remember the ones in the book are limited, you can add your own.

It is time to pray and confess these wrong behaviours, do it out loud.

PRAYER: Father God, I come to you to confess my sins. When I opened the door to fear, I also allowed many bad habits and wrong behaviours to enter my life. These behaviours are ………

………………………………………………………………………………

………………………………………………………………………………
I no longer want fear to control me and I do not desire to behave this way anymore. Holy Spirit help me change and create new

habits that are pleasing to you and helpful to me. Please forgive me Lord and wash me clean. In Jesus name, amen.

5. Change your self-talk

Changing our self-talk is hugely important. What comes out of our mouths is far more powerful than we commonly understand. We create or break our atmosphere with our words and we set our thinking patterns with our frequently spoken words as well. You will have subconsciously created many bad habits with your self-talk. Now you can use your self-talk to aid you in your recovery to freedom by speaking out the truth and the Word of God instead of what you feel and fear.

> *Likewise, the tongue is a small part of the body, but it makes great boasts. Consider what a great forest is set on fire by a small spark.*
>
> *The tongue also is a fire, a world of evil among the parts of the body. It corrupts the whole body, set's the whole course of one's life on fire, and is itself set on fire by hell...*
>
> *With the tongue we praise our Lord and Father, and with it we curse human beings, who have been made in God's likeness.*
>
> James 3:5, 6, 9

If you do not change your negative self-talk you will undo the good work you are doing in your life right now. God created everything with His words and we need to realise that we have been created to do the same, for good or for bad. Choose this day to work towards allowing only positive and encouraging words about yourselves and others to come out of your mouth. It takes time to break and create these habits, but if you are fully committed, you will experience an exciting and powerful new way of life.

- What kind of negative self-talk do you struggle with?
- Are you keen to make the change to being more positive?
- How do you plan on doing this?

TOOL: FEAR EVICTION PLAN
Page 130 in the back of this book

This plan will help you target your fears and negative self-talk. This is how it works…
- Pray and ask God to help you.
- Put in the date.
- Write in the challenge you are facing. Negative self-talk, fear or bad behaviour that you want to change.
- Write down the lie and then the truth. If you need help with this, ask a safe person.
- Put in a scripture that encourages you specifically in this area.
- Write in the 'Action' you are taking i.e. Instead of saying "I am hopeless at this" I will say, "I'm getting better at this."
- Do not fill out the last column until you have noticed you have completely changed your habit.

If you use this plan well, over time you will be able to see how many bad habits of fear, negative self-talk and wrong behaviours you have evicted. Then you should celebrate!!!

Chapter 7:

Weapons of Warfare

God does not expect us to fight a battle on our own or without weapons; He has fully resourced us. The weapons He has given us are very powerful!

> *"...No weapon formed against you will prevail, and you will refute every tongue that accuses you. This is the heritage of the servants of the Lord, and this is their vindication from me," declares the Lord.*
>
> Isaiah 54:17

God has endowed us with the most powerful equipment in the universe to ensure we prevail. When it comes to fear we are not fighting a natural battle but a spiritual one. The lies were planted by our spiritual enemy, the devil, who works to steal the truth, kill the soul and destroy our future. But there is no need to be afraid of him as Jesus has already dealt to him. Our role is to remind him of who we are as children of God and what Jesus has already conquered on our behalf. When we believe that our God will deliver us, the devil is unable to have his way and we can take back the freedom that is rightfully ours.

> *The weapons we fight with are not the weapons of the world. On the contrary they have divine power to demolish strongholds.*

> *We demolish arguments and every pretension that sets itself up against the knowledge of God, and we take captive every thought to make it obedient to Christ.*
> 2 Corinthians 10:4, 5

In Christ, we are stronger than we think we are!

'Finally, be strong in the Lord and in His mighty power. Put on the full armour of God, so that you can take your stand against the devil's schemes. For our struggle is not against flesh and blood, but against the rulers, against the authorities, against the powers of this dark world and against the spiritual forces of evil in the heavenly realms. Therefore, put on the full armour of God, so that when the day of evil comes, you may be able to stand your ground, and after you have done everything, to stand.
Ephesians 6:10-13

The weapons of our warfare are:

1. **Belt of TRUTH:**

> *Stand firm then, with the belt of truth buckled around your waist....*
> Ephesians 6:14

Truth is a very powerful part of our armour and a wonderful weapon to wield at the enemy. It exposes truth and it will keep us strong. We take the lies the enemy has been telling us and compare it with the truth in the Word of God. In other words, we expose the lie with what is 'actual.' With the belt of truth in place we are protecting ourselves from the devil's deceit.

> *".... if you hold to my teaching, you are really my disciples. Then you will know the truth and the truth will set you free."*
> John 8:31-32

When lying thoughts enter your head, or someone says or does something that is not true and not helpful, you must immediately respond in your heart with the truth. Do not entertain these lies or give them any space in your mind. If you do not know what the truth is, ask a safe person or check out the Word of God. Be honest to yourself. Tell yourself what you would say to someone you are helping.

Stress used to be a major battle for me. Now when I start feeling stressed thinking my work load is too difficult and heavy, I pray for God's help and then write down all the jobs that have to be done. I divide everything into order of importance and make a list of things that are priority for today. I tick them off as I go and almost every time, I manage to complete all or most of the tasks. The issue was more the fact that I was afraid of not having enough time, rather than the worry that I was running out of hours to get it all done.

We must tighten the belt of truth and leave no room for the lies of the enemy who is looking for opportunities to plant fear into our hearts and minds. Let truth be the mirror that exposes, the gauge that measures and the judge that rules. Hold fast to the truth and you will be free.

2. Breastplate of RIGHTEOUSNESS

The breastplate covers and protects your heart. In the natural, your heart is a life-giving organ and it needs significant protection. Your core emotions, your feelings, heart, mood and temperament, also need significant protection.

> *Stand firm then...with the breastplate of righteousness in place....*
> Ephesians 6:14

Righteousness is a powerful force in our world of sin. The verses below explain perfectly well how important it is to determine to be a decent, honest and loving human being. Righteousness, being the breastplate in our armoury, protects us from the enemy's arrows to our heart, for when we sin we are unprotected.

> *Kings detest wrongdoing, for a throne is established through righteousness*
> Proverbs 16:12

A throne includes power and authority and the dominion is established in righteousness. An upright and sinless life protects us from the enemy and secures our life forever with Christ Jesus.

> *Whoever pursues righteousness and love, finds life, prosperity and honour.*
> Proverbs 21:21

We need to be determined to put our wrong behaviours behind us and pursue Jesus; this involves new habit-forming efforts. We could never be good enough, but Jesus took our place on the cross, He defeated sin and death and then handed us His own righteousness and made us worthy.

> *Righteousness guards the person of integrity, but wickedness overthrows the sinner.*
> Proverbs 13:6

3. Gospel of PEACE:

> *...and with your feet fitted with the readiness that comes from the gospel of peace*
> Ephesians 6:15

In this verse we are encouraged to fit our feet with the gospel of peace. When our feet are fitted with this weapon, we have peace and we are ready to share it. Only Jesus has peace for us, a peace that actually works, a peace that exceeds our earthly understanding. His peace is the right fit for us. We must put it on and keep it on. It will be completely personalised for us; it will equip us to do the work of the Kingdom.

To be completely peaceful with a sound mind, we need to hand over all our cares and concerns to Jesus, fixing our eyes on Him and trusting He will take care of all things. The salvation that Christ purchased for us through His death and resurrection not only determines the long-term picture for us, but also the short term: We have peace for eternity and peace right now for our daily lives. There is nothing to big or small for God, He will take care of it all. His peace enables us to walk the road of life with confidence.

> *The fruit of righteousness will be peace; its effect will be quietness and confidence forever.*
> Isaiah 32:17

> *You will keep in perfect peace those whose minds are steadfast,*

because they trust in you.
Isaiah 26:3

We can really help ourselves by purposely choosing to think about things that are helpful and healthy for our minds. When we allow our minds to wander and don't use any restraint, we will be unable to rest and trust that God has it all under control.

Finally, brethren, whatever is true, whatever is honourable, whatever is right, whatever is pure, whatever is lovely, whatever is of good repute, if there is any excellence and if anything worthy of praise, dwell on these things.
Philippians 4:8

When we do not have peace, we are held back from our daily living and from doing what God has called us to do. Isaiah 26:3 tells us to hand over all our fears, worries, anxieties and cares to God and to keep our minds on Him.

Some of your thoughts are not healthy thoughts, some thoughts are sinful ones. Have you noticed that you are less peaceful when you sin? When you sin with your mind, it is actually sin, confess it and deal with it quickly.

Sometimes we need to give ourselves some basic tough love and just stop doing what we are doing. Start doing what is helpful and leave what is not helpful behind, move on! You are the only one who can turn off the record player in your head, so take control and put your mind onto something good and right!

- How are you going to make sure you are fitting your feet with the gospel of peace?
- What impact could you have on others when you are <u>not</u> walking in peace?
- What is the difference when you <u>are</u> walking in peace?
- How is heavens peace different than the worlds?

Pray this out-loud now as you confess…

PRAYER: Dear Heavenly Father, thank you that you care about everything that I am concerned about. Right now, I am concerned about many things and I choose to hand these things over to you

……………………………………………………………………………………

and I ask that you will take care of them. In Jesus' name amen.

4. Shield of FAITH

In addition to all this, take up the shield of faith, with which you can extinguish all the flaming arrows of the evil one.

Ephesians 6:16

I love the visual we get here, with faith being our shield, the piece of armour that covers and protects all the life-giving organs in our upper body. Faith is a very powerful weapon. We are often unaware of how powerful our faith is. The devil knows its power, but he loves to keep us ignorant or forgetful about its effectiveness.

We can see in the verse, that there is something for us to do. We must take up the shield of faith. This means we must proactively pick it up, put it on, wear it and use it.

> *… for everyone born of God overcomes the world. This is the victory that has overcome the world; even our faith.*
> 1 John 5:4

> *…. This inheritance is kept in heaven for you, who through faith are shielded by God's power until the coming of the salvation that is ready to be revealed in the last time.*
> 1 Peter 1:4-5

Fear can make things appear so much bigger than they actually are, almost as if we are looking at our situation through a magnifying glass. Faith in God brings our fear back to actual size. We can then look at our circumstance through God's eyes and with His perspective. With God, all things are possible.

This is what Jesus said to His disciples:

> *"…With man this is impossible, but not with God; all things are possible with God."*
> Mark 10:27

If we are lacking in faith, how do we increase this necessary and powerful weapon? Ask God to increase your faith. Be a diligent daily reader of the Word of God and you will find that faith will build in your heart. Speaking our faith out loud also increases our faith, this is called declaration. Sometimes we need to declare before we believe. When we declare we are also speaking it into the spiritual realm and that is very powerful. God spoke the world into being, so imagine what you can do with your faith!

> *.... faith comes from hearing the message, and the message is heard through the word about Christ.*
> Romans 10:17

- ❖ How can you increase your faith? Romans 10:17
- ❖ How powerful is your faith? Why is it powerful? 1 John 5:4
- ❖ What do you think it means, to extinguish all the flaming arrows of the evil one? Ephesians 6:16

5. Helmet of SALVATION

> *Take the helmet of salvation....*
> Ephesians 6:17

This weapon covers and protects your head. Our heads are very vulnerable physically and they are emotionally and spiritually as well. Here again, we are told to put the weapon on. What good will it be to us if we are not wearing it?

It is our salvation that confirms our true status as children of God. Because we are part of God's family, we have an inheritance that the enemy is unable to dislodge. If we immerse our mind and our thought life with the knowledge of what God has done for us, we can rest knowing we have security now and for eternity.

We understand the importance of knowing our earthly family and who we belong to. But it is also important to know you have a heavenly family, who they are and what they are like. Discover who you are in Christ. Don't be an acquaintance, don't just be a friend, be family. Partake in the relationship.

> But since we belong to the day, let us be sober, putting on faith and love as a breastplate and the hope of salvation as a helmet. For God did not appoint us to suffer wrath but to receive salvation through our Lord Jesus Christ.
> 1 Thessalonians 5:8, 9

6. WORD OF GOD

> ...and the sword of the spirit which is the Word of God
> Ephesians 6:17

I have always known and believed that God's Word is powerful, but it wasn't until I was quite unwell and desperate for freedom, that I used it specifically to target the enemy.

I used this powerful weapon for the areas of my mind the enemy had gained ground in, and the habits of fear I had allowed to form. On a daily basis, I declared Bible truth out loud to change my thought life, my self-talk and to create a positive truthful atmosphere for me to live in. I declared specifically chosen verses every day for months.

My spirit was empowered and encouraged as it aligned with the truth. When I started doing this I didn't feel anything, it was just an action I had chosen to do. But the more I did it the more I believed what I was declaring, to the point where the truth of God's Word felt alive and active in me. I actually remember the moment that I noticed a breakthrough in my spirit and in my heart. Things were different from then on and the devil most definitely had less ground in my life. I was beginning to win and since then I have been winning a lot!

> For the Word of God is alive and active. Sharper than any double-edged sword, it penetrates even to dividing soul and spirit, joints and marrow; it judges the thoughts and attitudes of the heart.
> Hebrews 4:12

So, the goal here is to choose the scriptures that will help you fight your fear situation. There are many at the back of this book. You can open your Bible or search on a Bible app just like you do on Google. Print them or write them out in large print and put them on your fridge, back of your doors and in your office. Learn them by heart and start to declare them out loud a few times a day. You need to keep this going for at least two months, but I encourage you to go longer and to not give up. If you give up you will miss out on your breakthrough point. I can guarantee that if you stick with it, things will start to change. Do not underestimate the power of God's Word. It is above and beyond what you could imagine!

> But whoever looks intently into the perfect law that gives freedom, and continues in it –

> *not forgetting what they have heard,*
> *but doing it – they will be blessed in what they do.*
> James 1:25

Take a moment to read Matthew 4:1-11 where you can see that Jesus was led by the Spirit into the wilderness to be tempted by the devil. He had fasted forty days and nights when the tempter arrived. Jesus used the Word of God to combat His enemy who left after three attempts.

7. **PRAYER**

> *And pray in the spirit on all occasions*
> *with all kinds of prayers and requests.*
> *With this in mind, be alert and always keep on*
> *praying for all the Lord's people.*
> Ephesians 6:18

Praying is just having a conversation with God. He is your heavenly father and He is always ready to hear from you. Pray all the time about everything and be specific. Be committed to prayer and believe that God has heard you and answered you. Find the scriptures that address your fears, your situation and pray them out loud over yourself and through your home.

> *The prayer of a righteous person*
> *is powerful and effective.*
> James 5:16

If our prayers are so powerful and effective why wouldn't we pray? Pray that God will give you the strength you need to stand firm and to hold onto your faith. Pray for a revelation of what Jesus has done for you, or whatever it is you sense you need.

> *Do not be anxious about anything, but in every situation, by prayer and petition, with thanksgiving, present your requests to God.*
> Philippians 4:6

Before you allow anxiety to take over your emotions, PRAY! At all times evaluate your emotions and do not give them free reign. You always have the opportunity to choose your response and your emotion. Decide how you want to feel and what atmosphere you want to live in. Make sure you make the most of this choice, evaluate and manage it effectively.

> *Therefore, I tell you, whatever you ask for in prayer, believe that you have received it, and it will be yours.*
> Mark 11:24

Approach

The true story of David and Goliath in 1 Samuel 17 is a great one to read when you are in the middle of a spiritual battle. Even though the Israelites had fought and won many battles before, they feared the potential outcome of this one would be vastly different because the philistine soldier was a narcissistic giant. Goliath came out every day for forty days, taking his stand and asking for an Israelite to fight him. No one responded day after day as they were all too afraid. David was just a young shepherd boy who loved God. What he did have as an advantage, was that he had fought and killed many wild animals while looking after his father's sheep. David chose to go out and face Goliath with no physical armour, but he did stand before the philistine giant with profound faith that the Lord would deliver him, and the peace that God would protect him. The young man approached Goliath with just a sling and five smooth stones. You could imagine the soldiers laughing at such a thing, can't you? Here's what David said, as he fronted up to the evil giant.

David said to the Philistine, "You come against me with the sword and spear and javelin, but I come against you in the name of the Lord Almighty, the God of the armies of Israel, whom you have defied. This day the Lord will deliver you into my hands, and I'll strike you down and cut off your head. This very day I will give the carcasses of the Philistine army to the birds and the wild animals, and the whole world will know that there is a God in Israel.

All those gathered here will know that it is not by sword or spear that the Lord saves; for the battle is the Lord's, and He will give all of you into our hands."

1 Samuel 17:45-47

Wow, this is a great example of declaration, we need to follow David's example. We can approach our enemy knowing that our Lord is with us, will fight for us, help us and deliver us. We can approach the enemy with boldness, not with physical weapons but with spiritual ones, because we are not fighting against flesh and blood but against spiritual powers. The weapons we carry may not make us look intimidating or impressive. They may not even make us appear to be fit for battle. But when we walk wearing God's armour we know we have done everything and we can stand firm. And we can say who's name we come in out loud, just as David did. *"I come against you in the name of the Lord Almighty!"* Let the enemy hear you say it!

We come to you as we are,
afraid and grieved we're broken.
For you nothing is too hard,
nothing separates us from your love.

Established deep in your love,
we walk by peaceful streams.
Jesus you're always enough,
you sustain and strengthen us.

You restore, you rebuild,
you complete what you started in us.
You restore and fulfil,
God you're faithful to all that you promised.

You build us strong,
you make us brave.
We overcome because you restore and save.

Janene Forlong 2015

Chapter 8:

We withdraw from the distractions of this world,
and come boldly to your throne.
So grateful are we to find your arms are wide open,
dry and thirsty you call us home.

We withdraw from the thoughts that entangle,
we fix our eyes on you Lord.
So grateful are we to discover your truth
sets us free and calls us home.

You call us home; you call us home.
Your mercy draws us to your side.
To where your blood was poured out
those many years ago.
Your grace has called us home.

Janene Forlong 2015

Life is Beautiful!

The wonderful thing I discovered about being free is that life seems so much more beautiful. It's not that there aren't any difficulties now, but when I was living in fear I couldn't enjoy even the simple things in life. The food tastes better, the scenery is more delightful, holidays are extra restful, and I am really keen for adventure because I am finally free to enjoy. Now change is exciting instead of something I dread, I want to explore new things, think about new ideas and my hopes and dreams are so much bigger than ever before.

Even more personally, freedom for me means I can determine which thoughts are lies and which are truth. I am not afraid of men or more specifically men in authority. It means I can speak to people on the phone or face to face with ease and I can sing and speak in front of a crowd. I can drive cars that are unfamiliar to me, travel and go on holiday, relax and sleep in unfamiliar accommodation. I don't worry about my house while I'm away and I am able to be at peace knowing that God is taking care of all my loved ones.

I am content with who God has made me to be and I do not believe I need to impress any human being. I understand that whether others accept or reject me doesn't change who I am, how unique or valuable I am. There isn't anyone or anything that can change my destiny except for me. The plan that God has for me will take place when and how He has determined, as long as I am following Him.

I wish it didn't take me so long to get to this point in my life; I am like a little child biting at the bit to have my new toy, candy and adventure all at once right now! I know for sure that I am created for something special, and I don't have many years left to do those things but I am sure going to do all I can.

Remembering it is more important to BE, than to DO, is the

hardest part of freedom for me. I first need to be God's girl, and out of that will flow what He has for me to do. Meanwhile I enjoy the view, the tastes, smells and sounds so much more than ever before.

This is what my freedom is looking like, but yours and someone else's could look vastly different, depending on what tears held you captive.

Stay Free
To ensure freedom continues to rule, remember to stand firm:
- Do not entertain any lies that come your way.
- Pray constantly and discern the truth.
- Proactively choose NOT to take offence or allow negative thinking to have even five seconds of your time.
- Be content with who God has made you and what He has for you.
- Do not be ashamed of your journey, share it with others and use it to encourage them along their way.
- Evaluate your emotions and choose the emotion you want to have; you are in charge of how you feel and what atmosphere you want to live in.
- Keep yourself right with God, confess your sins.
- Trust in the Lord for everything, take Him at his word.
- Remember who you belong to, you are a child of God.

Which of these do you find the hardest to do and why?

It is for freedom that Christ has set us free. Stand firm, then, and do not let yourselves be burdened again by a yoke of slavery.
Galatians 5:1

Pursue Jesus

It was the Lord who first pursued us, and He is still pursuing us so shouldn't we pursue him too? The more we pursue and follow the Lord, the more we will know Him and be like Him. You generally become like the people you spend time with.

Develop and continue a healthy appetite for the Word of God, making sure you have a good meal of it every day. I recommend reading the whole Bible, book by book, and meditating on individual verses, especially in the New Testament. Believe God, take Him at His Word, expect Him to guide you every day in all you do.

So then, just as you received Christ Jesus as Lord,
continue to live your lives in Him,
rooted and built up in Him,
strengthened in the faith as you were taught,
and overflowing in thankfulness.
Colossians 2: 6, 7

Spend time in prayer just having a conversation with God about anything and everything. Deepen your relationship by worshiping Him and appreciating Him for who He is. Discover how you best connect with Jesus, play worship music, walk and pray or shut yourself away in a quiet place.

Remember to continually bow boldly before your Lords throne, pushing away all the worlds' distractions. Look into His eyes, the only eyes that make you feel peaceful and safe. This is the place I call 'home' in the song lyrics written at the beginning of this chapter. Drink in who Jesus is. Meditate on all He has done and achieved for us on the cross, and the incredibly powerful results of His resurrection that makes life so precious. You need to return to His side daily to be washed and cleansed from the day's doings. When you do so, you will be re-empowered once again to love Him and serve Him.

Thanksgiving is a very powerful and important part of praise; thank God for bringing you into freedom. Look how far you have come and show your appreciation to the one who brought you through.

> *"... I am the Lord, who made you holy and who brought you out of Egypt to be your God. I am the Lord."*
> Leviticus 22:32 - 33

In Ephesians 4, the Apostle Paul talks about the life we are called to live and he encourages us to make our life count for Jesus. Unless you want to go back to your own personal Egypt and be enslaved once more with fear, find out how God wants you to live and just do it. These verses are a good place for you to start:

As a prisoner for the Lord, then, I urge you to live a life worthy of the calling you have received. Be completely humble and gentle; be patient, bearing with one another in love. Make every effort to keep the unity of the Spirit through the bond of peace...

... You were taught, with regard to your former way of life, to put off your old self, which is being corrupted by its deceitful desires; to be made new in the attitude of your minds; and to put on the new self, created to be like God in true righteousness and holiness. Therefore, each of you must put off falsehood and speak truthfully to your neighbour, for we are all members of one body. "In your anger do not sin": Do not let the sun go down while you are still angry, and do not give the devil a foothold. Anyone

who has been stealing must steal no longer, but must work, doing something useful with their own hands, that they may have something to share with those in need. Do not let any unwholesome talk come out of your mouths, but only what is helpful for building others up according to their needs, that it may benefit those who listen. And do not grieve the Holy Spirit of God, with whom you were sealed for the day of redemption. Get rid of all bitterness, rage and anger, brawling and slander, along with every form of malice. Be kind and compassionate to one another, forgiving each other, just as in Christ God forgave you.

Ephesians 4: 1-3, 22-32

As we pursue Jesus and allow His perfect love to drive out fear and heal us, we begin to take on more and more of His divine nature. How wonderful God is in His planning and foresight. Our job is to surrender and let Him bring about a glorious result, we will not be at all disappointed.

> *There is no fear in love.*
> *But perfect love drives out fear,*
> *because fear has to do with punishment.*
> *The one who fears is not made perfect in love.*
>
> 1 John 4:18

The longer you live this God designed lifestyle the more you will understand what He is doing, or has already done in your life. Down the track we can look back and appreciate the value of all that He has achieved through the difficult times we have gone through. The more we surrender, the more He can complete His planned work. I love what God is doing in my life and the older I get the more I like myself, though I can definitely see where extensive work is still required.

Free to Live

You are now proactively learning to live the lifestyle that Jesus purchased for you, the one that God had designed for you even before the beginning of time. You will have had some wonderful encounters with Jesus through the revelation of His Word, and you are getting to know Him through a prayer relationship. You will have seen how powerful His Word is when you declare it over your life and circumstances. You will have seen answered prayers, Godly provision, fear backing down, faith building up and so much more. It is a beautiful life, isn't it!

> *Now the Lord is the Spirit,*
> *And where the Spirit of the Lord is,*
> *there is freedom.*
>
> 2 Corinthians 3:17

In Chapter 5, I wrote that "Freedom is the right to full access to life, as given and promised by God himself. The perfect design for us to have abundant life." So, you are now free to serve, free to give, to help and to have vision. And in your serving, helping, giving and having vision, there is no need to be afraid or anxious.

You do not need to compare yourself with others, fear you will be rejected or not measure up. You are worthy because Jesus has made you so, He loves you and has called you, He believes in you and the purpose He has destined you with. So, live with the knowledge of who you are in Christ and do not let any lie keep you from enjoying your place on earth as a child of God. You are destined for a supernatural life here and a marvellous home in heaven.

Interesting Thought

When we are consumed with numerous fears, we are constantly thinking about ourselves and our worries. When fear is ruling we are often self-centred, fear centred. Taking our eyes off ourselves and putting them onto Jesus, steers us away from anxious thoughts.

My Freedom Definition

Freedom is the right to full access to life as given and promised by God himself. The perfect design for us to have abundant life.

Write your own definition here…

....
....
....
....
....
....
....

I'm Yours

Now that I'm yours I know victory,
now I can love with a passion.
Fulfilled as I walk with a purpose
working out my salvation.

You chose me to live in your presence.
You chose me to walk in your way.
You chose me to enjoy all your benefits.
You chose me to love and obey.

You chose me before I chose you.
I am yours.

Janene Forlong

Chapter 9

Freedom and Responsibility

It's time to arise, it's time to shine.
Come up from the dust for you are mine.
Though you once were the dry bones,
I am the life and I am breathing on you.

It's time to awaken to open your eyes.
Come up from the depths, from death to life.
Though the darkness covers the earth,
I am the light and I am rising on you.

The old has passed the new has come,
and you are pledged to my conquering son.
Though the world knows not who I am,
You are the light; I am rising on you.

For your light has come like the radiance of the dawn.
I have rebuilt and restored you stronger than before.
My glory covers you my chosen one,
You carry the hope the world is looking for.
Janene Forlong 2015

Freedom Releases Power

When we have come to a place of freedom we have come into a new place of power. What do I mean by this?

What I have noticed is, as I journey more and more into freedom I find that I have increasing confidence, courage and stamina. My relationship with the Lord is also growing and I hear Him speak to me more. I pick up on what He is saying and do what He says to the best of my ability. I have been living for the Lord for a long time, but serving Him now is remarkably different as there is a kind of effortlessness. I believe God is blessing and empowering me in all that I do.

Some of this ease will also be because of the courage that has replaced the fear that once ruled me. It is amazing how fear used to sabotage my life; it would even interfere with any effort I made in doing good. It is not that everything is easy now because fear has been evicted, but I am no longer being held back. What I desire to achieve comes more easily and I am sure that God is enabling me and giving me the power to do what He wants me to do.

Power and Responsibility

> *...From everyone who has been given much,*
> *much will be demanded;*
> *and from the one who has been trusted much,*
> *much more will be asked.*
>
> Luke 12:48

I'm sure you will have heard of the ancient saying, "With great power comes great responsibility.' The monarchs of this world understand this phrase very well. They do not have the freedom to do as they personally desire; the kingdoms needs come before their own. They are born into privilege and therefore married to the responsibility.

And so, it is similar with us: we are children of God, heirs to the throne through Jesus our Lord and Saviour. Because we are in the family we have been empowered to achieve what God has predestined and called us to do. Of course, with this privileged position comes responsibility and the needs of the Kingdom must come before our own. The thing is though, while we are focused on doing what we are called to do God is busy taking care of us, providing for us and protecting us.

> *Live as free people,*
> *but do not use your freedom as a cover-up for evil;*
> *live as God's slaves*
>
> 1 Peter 2:16

This next verse from Isaiah, was speaking about Jesus when it was first written. I believe, that as we are the sons and daughters of God, we have the same calling.

> *The Spirit of the sovereign Lord is on me,*
> *because the Lord has anointed me to*
> *proclaim good news to the poor.*
> *He has sent me to bind up the broken hearted,*
> *to proclaim freedom for the captives*
> *and release from darkness for the prisoners...*
>
> Isaiah 61:1

It is time to share the freedom you have with others, show the extent of God's grace and love on your life to those who have yet to find peace. Remember to be understanding, patient and gracious to those who are still living as captives of fear. You have experienced this captivity and now you know freedom, you have been given much and so much is expected from you.

Now that I am free I see people in captivity everywhere, and I remember what it was like. I understand that when you are enslaved you cannot see anything else but your own poor state. Life revolved around me and how I felt about all the difficulties I faced. So, it is time to have grace for those that are captive, pray for them, love on them, and smile at them. Lead them to freedom so they too can enjoy the peace that comes with knowing they are God's well-loved child.

> *You, my brothers and sisters*
> *were called to be free.*
> *But do not use your freedom to indulge the flesh;*
> *rather, serve one another humbly in love.*
>
> Galatians 5:13

Even before I was free, I loved to read God's word and find out about all the promises He has made to us. I could pray for others but had trouble implementing the same faith for myself. Now I look back at the transformation that He has done in my life, I am excited about the journey and I desperately want others to experience the same. Now I can take hold of His promises in His Word, believe them and even see them. I can use the authority I have in Jesus' name, see changes take place in my life and others.

I used to be fearful and passive. Now I am bold and assertive in Jesus' name. I never used to speak up for myself or others when things weren't right, but now I do in love and without fear. Praise the Lord for His wonderful works. He has not only saved me for eternal life; He has given me a rich life on earth.

> *But thanks be to God,*
> *who always leads us as captives*
> *in Christ's triumphal process and*
> *uses us to spread the aroma of the knowledge*
> *of Him everywhere.*
>
> 2 Corinthians 2:14

- ❖ Why do we have more power when we have a new level of freedom?
- ❖ What did it mean for David, Esther and Moses?

David, Esther and Moses were not great people in their own right, it was God who made them great. They had fears, worries and concerns like any of us. Moses could hardly speak and David was just a boy. Esther was living in a time when Jews and women were not liberated, yet God used her to liberate her own people.

Moses, Esther and David faced their fears, God gave them victory and through that freedom they gained greater power? The more freedom you have, the more of God's power you have flowing through you.

- ❖ What is your understanding of the phrase, "With great power comes great responsibility?"
- ❖ What will you do with your new found freedom and power?

It's Time to Arise

Well done for all the effort you have put into evicting fear so far and thank you Jesus, for the freedom you are bringing to this life. You know what to do to get free from fear now, you know how to name the fears, evict them and move forward. It is important that you stay committed to the desire and process to get your freedom. Do not give up, do not quit. You have God's agreement for freedom so don't listen to the enemy when he tells you it is not working. You must remain submitted to the Holy Spirits prodding and trust that God will finish this wonderful work in you.

Remember

Continue with the tool box on page 121, the scripture declarations on page 123 and the fear eviction plan on page 129, which you are welcome to print. These are very powerful weapons and they will help you evict the enemy of fear. Ask the Holy Spirit to help you change your self-talk.

Remember…

- God did NOT give you a spirit of fear, but He DID give you love, power and a sound mind. Go deep into God's presence to allow His perfect love to wash over you and through you. When you are in His presence, focus and ask for His perspective and you will begin to see things differently. Lies will be exposed and the truth will be clear.

- To be bold and sensible with your gifts. Do not shy away from what God has called you to do. He has given you power to live life to the full and to continue to fight for freedom.

- It is more important to know how to be His child than to achieve great exploits for Him. Lean in to Him and breakthrough for an intimate relationship with Him.

- You will bring freedom to those around you. Help those who are going through a similar journey, share your successes and challenges with each other. Tell others what works for you so that it may help them, and listen for the encouraging advice that will come your way.

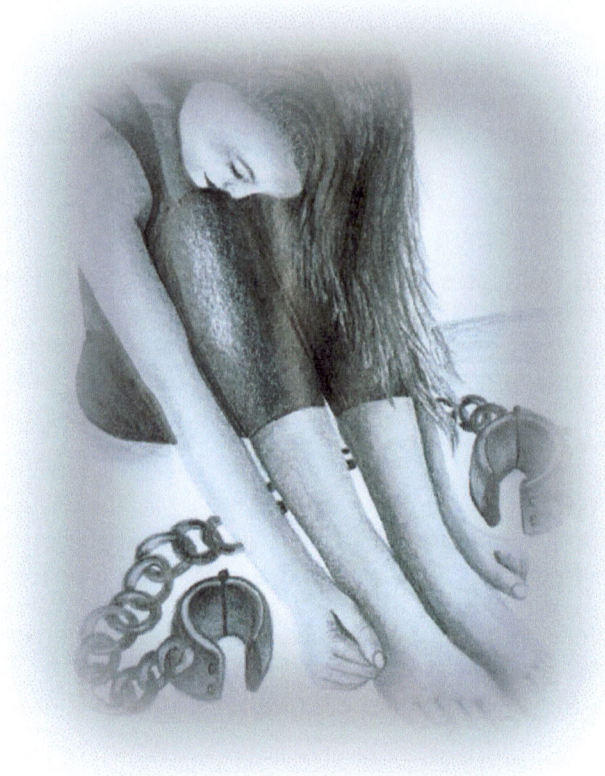

Do not accept the chains of fear any longer. Jesus paid for your freedom a long time ago. It is time to arise. Enjoy your freedom, your fearless living. There is always more freedom to be gained. Rise up and walk, become who you are destined to be, in Jesus' Name.

Your Reflections

Freedom Toolbox

1. Choose Freedom

- ❖ Tell God you want to be free.
- ❖ Be willing to let God do the work.

2. Believe in the name of Jesus

- ❖ Anything is possible for the one who believes.
- ❖ Partner with God and believe that He will deliver you.

3. Confess your fears

- ❖ Ask God to show you your fears.
- ❖ Write them down and call them what they are, e.g. lies of the enemy.
- ❖ Confess your fear as sin to God.
- ❖ Name the fears and renounce them in the name of Jesus.

PRAYER:
I renounce and resist the spirit of unbelief. I have decided that there is no longer a place in my mind, my heart or my life for unbelief and therefore I evict and command the spirit to leave right now, through the mighty power of Jesus name, amen.

PRAYER:
I renounce and resist the spirit of fear, in the name of Jesus. I have decided that there is no longer a place in my mind, my heart

or my life for any fear to rule. Therefore, I evict and command the fear of ....

.... to leave right now, through the mighty power of Jesus name, amen.

4. Identify wrong behaviours

- ❖ Prayerfully consider and write down the behaviours you use to support your fears.
- ❖ Confess these behaviours to God as sin.
- ❖ Ask the Lord to help you change the way you behave.

5. Change your self-talk

- ❖ Note when you use fearful language, negative talk.
- ❖ Ask the Lord to help you change what comes out of your mouth.

6. Weapons of Warfare

Put on the full armour of God Ephesians 6:6-10

- ❖ Truth: John 8:31-32
- ❖ Righteousness: Proverbs 21:21
- ❖ Peace of God: Isaiah 26:3
- ❖ Faith: Ephesians 6:16
- ❖ Salvation: 1 Thessalonians 5:8-10
- ❖ Word of God: Hebrews 4:12
- ❖ Prayer: James 5:16

Two Week Scripture Declaration Plan

Read and declare two verses out loud, as many times as possible each day, as planned below. Repeat fortnightly or create a new plan to span at least three months. A minimum of six weeks of declaration is recommended. The longer you commit the better the outcome.

Day 1

The thief comes only to steal and kill and destroy; 'I have come that they may have life, and have it to the full.'

John 10:10

Then he placed his right hand on me and said: 'Do not be afraid. I am the First and the Last.

Revelation 1:17

Day 2

Have I not commanded you? Be strong and courageous. Do not be terrified; do not be discouraged, for the Lord your God will be with you wherever you go.

Joshua 1:9

Keep your lives free from the love of money and be content with what you have, because God has said, "Never will I leave you; never will I forsake you." So, we say with confidence, "The Lord is my helper; I will not be afraid. What can mere mortals do to me?

Hebrews 13:5-6

Day 3

But now, this is what the Lord says, "Fear not, for I have redeemed you; I have summoned you by name; you are mine.

Isaiah 43:1

For God has not given us a spirit of fear, but of power and of love and of a sound mind.

2 Timothy 1:7

Day 4

When anxiety was great within me, your consolation brought joy to my soul.

Psalms 94:19

Even though I walk through the valley of the shadow of death, I will fear no evil, for you are with me; your rod and your staff, they comfort me.

Psalms 23:4

Day 5

Therefore, do not worry about tomorrow, for tomorrow will worry about itself. Each day has enough trouble of its own.

Matthew 6:34

Do not be anxious about anything, but in every situation, by prayer and petition, with thanksgiving, present your requests to God. And the peace of God, which transcends all understanding, will guard your hearts and your minds in Christ Jesus.

Philippians 4:6-7

Day 6

Humble yourselves, then, under God's mighty hand, so that He will lift you up in His own good time. Leave all your worries with Him, because he cares for you.

1 Peter 5:6-7

Peace is what I leave with you; it is my own peace that I give you. I do not give it as the world does. Do not be worried and upset; do not be afraid.

John 14:27

Day 7

Tell everyone who is discouraged, 'Be strong and don't be afraid! God is coming to your rescue...'

Isaiah 35:4

The Lord is with me; I will not be afraid. What can man do to me? The Lord is with me; He is my helper.

Psalms 118:6-7

Day 8

Do not worry about your life, what you will eat; or about your body, what you will wear. Life is more than food, and the body more than clothes. Consider the ravens: They do not sow or reap; they have no storeroom or barn; yet God feeds them. And how much more valuable you are than birds! Who of you by worrying can add a single hour to his life? Since you cannot do this very little thing, why do you worry about the rest?

Luke 12:22-26

Day 9

The Lord is my light and my salvation—whom shall I fear? The Lord is the stronghold of my life—of whom shall I be afraid?

Psalms 27:1

Immediately He spoke to them and said, 'Take courage! It is I, don't be afraid.

Mark 6:50

Day 10

Be strong and courageous. Do not be afraid or terrified because of them, for the Lord your God goes with you; He will never leave you nor forsake you.

Deuteronomy 31:6

And I am convinced that nothing can ever separate us from God's love. Neither death nor life, neither angels nor demons, neither our fears for today nor our worries about tomorrow—not even the powers of hell can separate us from God's love.

Romans 8:38-39

Day 11

For I am the Lord, your God, who takes hold of your right hand and says to you, 'Do not fear; I will help you. Do not be afraid, for I myself will help you,' declares the Lord, your Redeemer, the Holy One of Israel.

Isaiah 41:13-14

God is our refuge and strength, an ever-present help in trouble.

Psalms 46:1

Day 12

When I am afraid, I put my trust in you. In God, whose word I praise – in God I trust and am not afraid. What can mere mortals do to me?

Psalms 56:3,4

Do not be afraid of them; the Lord your God Himself will fight for you.

Deuteronomy 3:22

Day 13

Fear of man will prove to be a snare, but whoever trusts in the Lord is kept safe.

Proverbs 29:25

So do not fear, for I am with you; do not be dismayed, for I am your God. I will strengthen you and help you; I will uphold you with my righteous right hand.

Isaiah 41:10

Day 14

Whoever dwells in the shelter of the Most High will rest in the shadow of the Almighty. I will say of the Lord, "He is my refuge and my fortress, my God, in whom I trust."

Psalms 91:1, 2

"Because he loves me," says the Lord, "I will rescue him; I will protect him, for he acknowledges my name. He will call on me, and I will answer him; I will be with him in trouble, I will deliver him and honour him."

Psalms 91:14-15

FEAR EVICTION PLAN—WATCH OUTCOMES GROW OVER TIME!

START DATE				
FEAR				
LIE				
TRUTH				
ACTION				
SCRIPTURE				
OUTCOME & DATE				

References

All Scripture quotations, unless otherwise indicated, are taken from the Holy Bible, New International Version®, NIV®. Copyright ©1973, 1978, 1984, 2011 by Biblica, Inc.™ Used by permission of Zondervan. All rights reserved worldwide. www.zondervan.com The "NIV" and "New International Version" are trademarks registered in the United States Patent and Trademark Office by Biblica, Inc.™

Scripture quotations marked (AMP) are taken from the Amplified Bible, Copyright © 1954, 1958, 1962, 1964, 1965, 1987 by The Lockman Foundation. Used by permission.